THE
PITCHFORK
REVIEW

Collect Them All.

thepitchforkreview.com

Our contributors include Demi Adejuyigbe, Liz Armstrong, Welcome Emily Berl, Jefferson Cheng, Hazel Cills, Grayson Haver Currin, Meaghan Garvey, Joe Gross, Ian Harris, Jessica Hopper, Eleni Kalorkoti, Adam Kidron, Tim Lahan, to Sara Lautman, Zoë Leverant, J.R. Nelson, Marianna Ritchey, Issue Zak Sally, David Sampson, Scott Seward, Laura Snapes, Spot, Chris Stein, Estelle Tang, Ellen van Engelen, Carvell Wallace 6 & Brian Zarley.

T O O S N S

C O N T R O L P

The Pitchfork Review No. 6, Spring 2015. Published four times a year by Pitchfork Media Inc., 3317 W. Fullerton Ave., Chicago, IL 60647. All material © 2015. All rights reserved. Subscription rate in the US for 4 issues is $49.99. The Pitchfork Review is distributed by Publishers Group West. All advertising inquiries should be directed to Matthew Frampton at mattf@pitchfork.com. The Pitchfork Review does not read or accept unsolicited submissions, nor does it assume responsibility for the views expressed by its contributors. Contact info@thepitchforkreview.com for general information and reprints. Reproduction in whole or in part without permission is prohibited. The Pitchfork Review is a registered trademark of Pitchfork Media Inc.

Printed by Palmer Printing Inc. 739 S. Clark St., Chicago, IL 60605. Set in typefaces from Klim Type Foundry (klim.co.nz), Lineto (lineto.com), Colophon Foundry (colophon-foundry.org), Grilli Type (grillitype.com), and Mergenthaler. Printed on Mohawk Via and porcelainECO from Veritev.

ISBN 978-0-9913992-5-3

Ryan Schreiber
Founder & CEO

Chris Kaskie
President

Ryan Kennedy
Publisher

Jessica Hopper
Editor in Chief

Michael Catano
Deputy Editor

Stuart Berman
Senior Editor

Ryan Dombal
Mark Richardson
Brandon Stosuy
Contributing Editors

Oriana Leckert
Proofreader

Joseph Bidsziewski
Jr. Typist

Michael Renaud
Creative Director

Molly Butterfoss
Art Director

Joy Burke
Jessica Viscius
Graphic Design

Matthew Frampton
VP, Business

Megan Davey
VP, Finance

Charlotte Zoller
Social Media

RJ Bentler
VP, Video Programming

Brian Fitzpatrick
Logistics

Ash Slater
Events & Support

Matthew Dennewitz
VP, Product

Mark Beasley
Andrew Gaerig
Neil Wargo
Developers

ILLUSTRATION BY MOLLY BUTTERFOSS

I'm standing behind the lectern of a darkened high school auditorium in Grayslake, Illinois, talking to a room full of teens about how I have spent the last 19 years writing about songs and bands and ideas. Some kids fall asleep, others take notes—hopefully picking up whatever caustic wisdom I am laying down; suffice to say, it's no TEDxCentral High.

During the Q&A portion of the program, the questions are thoughtful and curious: some seek my opinion on the sundry works of Fall Out Boy, the Dead, and Chief Keef; others want to know if I get into Lollapalooza for free. I call on the raised hand of a young sir of the 11th grade, clad in a faded *Dark Side of the Moon* shirt who wants to quiz me about my hip-hop knowledge. I run down a quick list of likes—Mick Jenkins, Nicki, Eric B. & Rakim—and he responds with a "not bad" face, like I have surprisingly surpassed whatever low expectation he had for either my knowledge or taste.

I push down the impulse to clapback at the young dude, and in my half second pause I realize—standing there, under an actual-not-even-metaphorical spotlight—that as much as he is a real person in the right now, he's also an archetype. Sometimes he wears a Pink Floyd shirt. Sometimes he's in concert jazz band. Sometimes he's a mean hesher with a Slayer backpatch. But he is always bemused, shaking his head at whatever music you love that week, and he exists at every high school throughout the known universe. He is infinite and everlasting, and he has been there since the dawn of time. There is always *that dude*.

An hour later, I'm teaching a workshop to kids who are interested in music writing, and the way each of them talk about the songs they love (and hate) tenderizes my heart—the kid that identifies with Chicago-local struggle rappers; the boy that gets choked up talking about which Tegan & Sara songs helped him through a tough year; the totally normal-looking, 9th grade girl who is quiet until I ask what music means the most to her ("Godspeed You! Black Emperor?"); a girl that insists she listens to "nothing but Eagles albums," who dispenses incisive, off-the-dome pop criticism about the problematic paradigm of Megan Trainor. I clasp my hands together to keep from clapping giddily after each of them speaks.

It's a huge privilege to talk about writing and music with people who love those things as much as I do—nerding out with the other nerds about nerd shit, basically—and this is why it's so exciting for me to be a part of this magazine. High school remains as god awful as you remember it and teenagers are still assholes (sometimes), but they are also complete geniuses—and it's a beautiful thing. I hope one day they are running *The Pitchfork Review*, their good work dwarfing ours.

Jessica Hopper
Editor in Chief
April 7, 2015

flipbait

FLIPBAIT IS THE SECTION OF THE REVIEW FOR WHEN YOU'VE ALREADY REFRESHED INSTAGRAM AND TRIPLE-CHECKED YOUR FACEBOOK NOTIFICATIONS.

ILLUSTRATIONS BY **ELENI KALORKOTI**

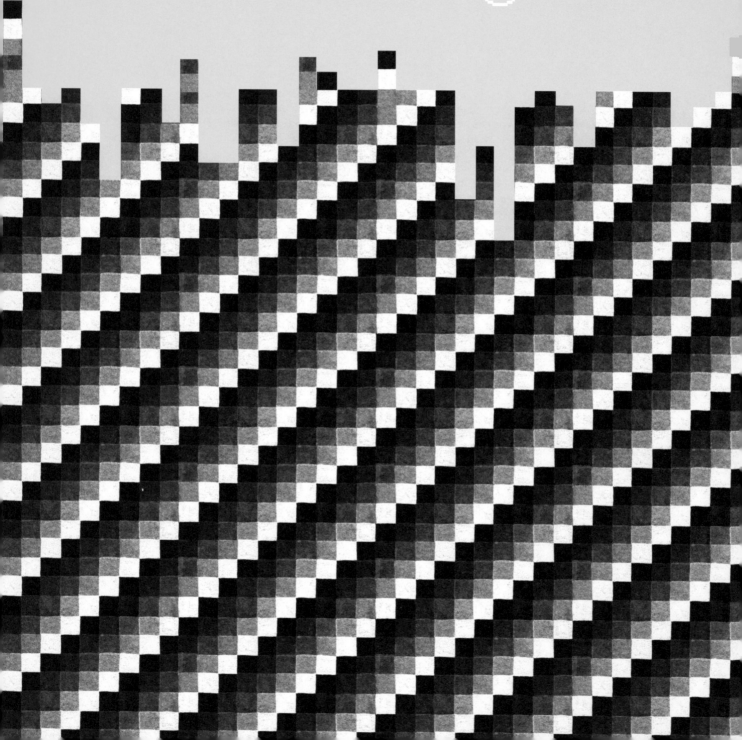

Side Eye Spectrum BY ESTELLE TANG

ONCE AGAIN, we take a look at the eyerolliest items in this great industry of music. People make mistakes, we get it! But which of our musician friends have made the most notably annoying boo-boos? Let's take a look and rank them from "not that okay" to "BLEIAGH."

gentle sidelong glance

"Catfish and the Bottlemen."

Juxtaposing "iconic" and "ironic" in lyrics: Thank you for being a friend, Madonna. A friend of rhymes.

This genius.com annotation on "Feelin' Myself": "Beyoncé and Nicki Minaj are at the top of their game—feeling themselves is an understatement. Both artists have millions of fans feeling every moment with them." Feelings, so many feelings.

Did you know that there's a YouTube video of Panic! at the Disco doing a cover of "Karma Police"? Now you do.

Peak Media Kanye-centrism: I almost forgot to care about gutkicker "All Day" because I left Gives Fucks Town after avoiding Grammy thinkypieces and his lackluster Adidas collab.

Corey Taylor's third book is called *You're Making Me Hate You*. It's about stuff the Slipknot singer doesn't like. Come on, dude, just use Twitter—or a line chart in *The Pitchfork Review*, haha.

Britpop Resurgence (kind of): New albums by Noel Gallagher and Blur. Y'all ready for this? Guys? Hello? Also, the writing on the cover of said Blur album is in Asian Chinese. Actually, so is most of the writing in the "hilarious karaoke Chinese cooking show" video for the single "Go Out!" Nnngh, it's not ACTUALLY the '90s. I'm so tired, you guys.

Ew factor: Critic Robert Christgau spent one-ninth of his "Expert Witness" review of *No Cities to Love* surmising which Sleater-Kinney members can bank.

Worst thing about Chris Brown, Tyga, and Schoolboy Q's "Bitches N Marijuana": the "I dick your bitch down" line or its piercingly hi-freq vocal riff? I don't know! I GUESS IT ALL TAKES THE POOP CAKE.

giant eyeball rolling around forever

What Your Favorite Radiohead Song Says About You BY DEMI ADEJUYIGBE

ALL I NEED: Multiple people are worried you might kill them.

KARMA POLICE: "Nice party, man. Is that your guitar? You guys know 'Time of Your Life'?"

CREEP: You wouldn't trade your job as a radio emcee for anything in the world!

FAKE PLASTIC TREES: Someone made fun of you when you chose "Creep."

STOP WHISPERING: You're torn between a Tommy Bahama addiction and paying for your kids' college.

KNIVES OUT: Everyone is sick of hearing you talking about your ex.

TREEFINGERS: You've lost count of how many times you've been to Joshua Tree.

STREET SPIRIT: You've got a "go-to" karaoke song that has been chosen mainly to get you complimented.

KID A: You're very comfortable being patronizing to anyone younger than you.

SEPARATOR: You subscribe to multiple podcasts about meditation.

MYXOMATOSIS: Your friends are lying when they say you're a great dancer.

RECKONER: You're cool and smart and handsome and you wrote a fantastic article for *The Pitchfork Review*. Everyone loves it.

BODYSNATCHERS: Every employee at Guitar Center knows you by name.

PARANOID ANDROID: "I'm just saying, the Beatles are lucky they got to music before Radiohead did."

Bjork's Mother's Day Gift Guide

gleðileg vor!
the flowers are escaping their vacation homes in the ground
the earth is spinning away from the sun, in defiance of the stars
the hallmark store is filled with hurried fathers and their children
mother's day is here once more

but what gift can match the gift of life?
a picnic basket, each food a memory of growth
a jar of sand, each grain a laugh from mother to child
an electric blanket, charged with nine months of battery life
today, i am your shepherd through the amazon wish list of the heart

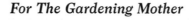

For The Gardening Mother

a vase, glass-blown in the contour of a teardrop
a grab bag of seeds, each a plant that symbolically births another seed
a sharpened spade, with which to fight any giant atop of the beanstalk

For The Electronic Mother

a synthesizer, backlit with color to induce synesthesia
a digitally-connected thermostat, monitoring and adjusting to her body warmth
a copy of *dancer in the dark*, on blu-ray 3-d

For The Artistic Mother

a collection of her art, mounted and bound in a coffee table book
a wooden easel, carved from a tree she kissed beneath as a child
a custom portrait of your birth, painted in
months of collected blood and tears

For The Musical Mother

a theremin, to craft music with her motions
a tour for two of the automatic instruments on display at
siegfried's mechanical music museum in rüdesheim, germany
a second theremin, to replace the first if it breaks

For The Offbeat Mother

a vial of your blood,
collected in a synthetic gemstone necklace
a taxidermied rodent, mounted and encased in glass
a cotton-stuffed doll with the visage of jenny's mother from
down the street, pins in all her limbs

For The Cooking Mother

a cookbook of updated ancient recipes
an egg timer in the shape of your bronzed baby shoes
an apron proclaiming that its wearer is due a kiss for
her irish heritage

For The Mother On The Go

a bicycle with a metal frame recycled from an old table
a leather laptop bag, made from the hide of a cow on her father's farm
a travel mug, emblazoned with a warning of the dangers of conversation
before she has consumed her morning caffeine

—CHANNELED BY DEMI ADEJUYIGBE

fl

Whose Cut Is the Deepest?

A LOOK AT THE WORLD OF ANGLED TRESSES.

BY ZOË LEVERANT

JONNY GREENWOOD

A hair legend in his own right, Greenwood's locks are as sharp as his guitar strings and as bleakly efficient as his score for *There Will Be Blood*. **COULD CUT: MOST FRUITS AND VEGETABLES (INCLUDING PINEAPPLES), GLASS ON A GOOD DAY**

ROBYN

Her sleek style's likely standard on the Fembots-only perma-party planet she undoubtedly calls home, but to mere earthlings it's a magnificent wonder to behold. **COULD CUT: STRAIGHT THROUGH THE FABRIC OF THE UNIVERSE, BUT SHE'S HAVING WAY TOO MUCH FUN TO TRY**

DANNY BROWN

His wispy yet substantial droop personifies the rhymes that hooked the world: weird, irreverent, complex, and absolutely impossible to ignore. **COULD CUT: ELECTRICAL WIRING, SINCE IT LOOKS LIKE IT'S SURVIVED A FEW SHOCKS ALREADY**

KAREN O

That unnervingly glossy halo seems like it's hiding some secrets underneath, including the exact date of the last time Nick Zinner washed his own unmistakeable 'do. **COULD CUT: ALMOST ANY CLOTH, ESPECIALLY THE NEON AND/OR SPARKLY VARIETY**

ROMY CROFT

"Precocious" is a lofty description for a hairstyle, and her unusual shape perfectly communicates a woman short on age but long on insight and talent. **COULD CUT: A MODEST STACK OF *NME* BACK ISSUES**

OWEN PALLETT

By sheer force of talent (or is it handsomeness?), Mr. Final Fantasy turns the horrible early-aughts emo fringe swoop into pure refinement and mystery. **COULD CUT: BUTTER THAT'S BEEN SITTING OUT FOR A WHILE, BUT NOT MUCH ELSE**

**SCENE REPORTS
FROM ANTIQUITY**
BY MARIANNA RITCHEY

Neither First nor Last

The price of Clara Schumann's genius

Life in a patriarchy is crummy in all manner of ways, but one of the more subtle yet insidious of these, I have found, is the way that the system requires every woman who does something cool to be "the first." In music history we face a similar bind: we must somehow simultaneously believe that women have never been serious musicians or composers, while also studying and teaching all manner of serious female musicians and composers. Elisabeth Jacquet de la Guerre, Barbara Strozzi, Francesca Caccini, Fanny Mendelssohn—the list goes on. (The goddamn first composer whose name we actually have attached to her works is a woman! Her name was Hildegard, she lived 1,000 years ago, and her music is so beautiful that scholars use it to demonstrate how the values of humanism were rising in Europe long before the Renaissance. Give me a break!) These women are in all the textbooks, and yet we are also instructed to mournfully shake our heads at the fact that women have not been allowed to contribute to the history of arts and letters. This is not to say that women in history had it easy, as their lives were obviously a revolting slog most all of the time; I'm saying that they were there, and they did stuff, and pretending they didn't—even sympathetically! Even to prove a point about how much you hate sexism!—is crap.

Clara Schumann was one of these women from music history who felt she was "the first" even though she wasn't, and who suffered for it. Born Clara Josephine Wieck in 1819 in Leipzig, she was a child prodigy whose precocious skill at the piano made her internationally famous by the time she was a preteen. Kings and queens brought her to play for them and loaded her with fabulous gifts. She toured the world with her strange and domineering father (has there been a child prodigy in history who hasn't had a strange and domineering parent?), who raised her according to the extremely weird child-rearing principles laid out by Rousseau in *Emile*, meaning that Clara was taught very little aside from piano technique.

She was driven, self-confident, and pretty much wholly devoted to music, except for her early teen years, when her father complained that she had become boy-crazy. Indeed, she went against her father's direct orders and married the composer-slash-journalist Robert Schumann, which her father had forbidden.

Beginning the day after their wedding, Clara and Robert kept a joint diary, which is now a priceless historic document. They took turns writing in it, trading off each week. Reading the entries, the tone of mutuality and respect apparently expected within their marriage is striking. Indeed, Robert writes in the first entry, "One of the highlights of our little diary...will be the criticism of our artistic accomplishments; e.g., what you have been studying especially, what you are composing, what new things you have learned, and what you think about them will be entered in detail; the same holds for me."

Robert had a famously difficult life and deeply tragic death, yet as one reads the diaries it is often Clara's difficulties that resonate the strongest. She's an artist, and she's lucky enough to be married to a guy who (most of the time) thinks it's cool that she's an artist, but she's also a nineteenth-century wife, and that brings with it certain responsibilities and even a depressing mode of self-denigration in which she's forever berating herself for being so lazy or for angering Robert or for not being able to focus on her work because of household chores. And yet she continues to persevere. She composes, she practices, she goes on yet another international concert tour. She writes elegant criticism of the various Italian operas she is forced to sit through. Despite her guilt over not being as good a wife as she ought, she keeps on trucking.

In spite of her eight children and her degenerating husband—he struggled his whole life with mental illness, and ultimately committed himself to an institution after a failed suicide attempt—Clara continued touring internationally as a very respected pianist, earning the lion's share of the family income, thus fulfilling her father's evil promise that if she married against his wishes she would be impoverished and overworked, left to care single-handedly for a bevy of dreaded children. Imagine having your seventh child and then hopping out of bed and riding in a horse-drawn carriage to Paris to play Beethoven bagatelles for princes and philistines! The mind reels.

Given the perhaps surprising coolness of their marriage, certain diary entries do give one the howling fantods, not only because of patriarchy but also because of the peculiar insanity of German Romanticism in music. Robert is forever telling Clara that she should not put so much of herself into her performance of his works, for that would be like a painter insisting he had made a better tree than God. Or, for example, here is Clara:

> We have started with the Fugues of Bach; Robert marks those places where the theme always returns—studying these fugues is really quite interesting and gives me more pleasure each day. Robert reprimanded me very strongly; I had doubled one place in octaves, and thus impermissibly added a fifth voice to the four-voice texture. He was right to denounce this, but it pained me not to have sensed it myself.

I can vividly picture this scene; Robert looming over her shoulder, jabbing angrily at the page with one of his deformed fingers.

The fingers! At one point, seeking to liberate his right ring finger from his middle finger, he used some sort of machine, perhaps one intended to stretch various ligaments. Tragically, the machine ruined his hand in some ambiguous way no one can quite define, and so his performing career was over.

> **She was alone; she was trying to do something unprecedented. She was "the first" and didn't want to be, so she quit.**

In the 1830s–1850s it was becoming increasingly imperative for composers to perform their own works onstage, so that they could demonstrate all the authentic "music trances" and emotional engagement with their art that were becoming required as proof that they were a *true artist*. With this avenue now closed forever, Robert increasingly turned to Clara as his voice or, more accurately, as his literal right hand. Clara became the most dependable interpreter of his work; he spoke through her and came to rely on her as his only means of showing audiences what his pieces ought to sound like. Their relationship, as you can imagine, was intense. Clara felt a heavy responsibility not only to her husband, but to Art itself.

To this day she remains one of the most famous performing virtuosos in all of music history, but she also played the not insignificant role of helping to shape and cultivate a whole scene of composers. If she played one of your works in public, it could skyrocket you to fame. She was a major mover and shaker in European music post-Beethoven. Her music was straight-up good, and every bit as meaningful as her husband's. She played and played, but, in the face of journalists declaring her works to be, at worst, incompetent, and, at best, good but overly feminine, she slowly lost the will to compose.

Here she is, at age 36: "I once believed that I possessed creative talent, but I have given up this idea; a woman must not desire to compose—there has never yet been one able to do it. Should I expect to be the one?" Just as we are cut off from her today, she herself was cut off from the other women of music history. She couldn't see herself in the lineage of Caccini or Strozzi or the myriad female composers of the eighteenth century. She was alone; she was trying to do something unprecedented. She was "the first" and didn't want to be, so she quit. After Robert died, she stopped composing, focusing on her career as a performer. Which is nothing to sniff at! But it is the realm of performance that has historically been more welcoming to women than the world of composition.

It has become an outdated truism in rock music that women have no role models, no example of what it would look like for a woman to pick up a guitar and shred, for example. But this perceived lack—just like Schumann's—has more to do with the way history is written than with women's actual contributions to all genres of music, which have for centuries been significant and multifarious. Because we live in a system that teaches us that each woman we encounter, in any era, must bear the burden of being "the first" or "the only," our histories get written in such a way that all these fruitful lineages are broken, and we have to keep rediscovering them again and again.

SPRING EDITION
BY J.R. NELSON

Circulation Desk

J.R. Nelson examines the effluvia of Robert Christgau's rock-crit memoir

Critic and editor Robert Christgau has been there from the very beginning, notoriously (and/or jokingly) referring to himself as the Dean of American Rock Critics since the early '70s. It's a testament to his longevity and standing that the boast hasn't lost the ring of truth. Never the most indulgent of critics, even his earliest and more reported longform pieces from the peace/love/dope–soaked '60s for *Esquire* and *Newsday* (grab a copy of his collection *Any Old Way You Choose It* to read them) are soft on narrative and contain more than a few traces of the master's fearsome imperiousness. The brevity and rhetorical snap of his most epochal work, the Consumer Guide reviews for the *Village Voice* and his exhaustive '70s, '80s, and '90s by-decade record guides (including report card letter grades), has long entertained music obsessives, and for good reason. Rooting around these short reviews—in short doses as inspired—almost always offers immediate pleasure. Here he is, putting the treatment on my favorite album, by The Replacements:

Let It Be [Twin/Tone, 1984]
Those still looking for the perfect garage may misconstrue this band's belated access to melody as proof they've surrendered their principles. Me, I'm delighted they've matured beyond their strange discovery of country music. Bands like this don't have roots, or principles either, they just have stuff they like. Which in this case includes androgyny (no antitrendie reaction here) and Kiss (forgotten protopunks). Things they don't like include tonsillectomies and answering machines, both of which they make something of. A+

These methods have often infuriated rock stars. Lou Reed was moved to call the Dean a "toe fucker" on a live album—surely a mark of pride for any critic. As Thurston Moore of Sonic Youth complained on "I Killed Christgau With My Big Fucking Dick":

I don't know why
You wanna impress Christgau
Ah let that shit die
And find out the new goal

What fan of music writing wouldn't want to read a memoir about a "toe fucker" who pisses off Thurston Moore? Robert Christgau's new memoir, *Going into the City: Portrait of a Critic as a Young Man,* is that book: a mash note to New York City, to his discovery of sexual love and his quest for monogamy and family, and to his life of ideas regarding pop music. The smashing together of big and small events can make for exhaustion and bewilderment to the lonely reader sifting for insights, and in this book there are some choppy waters right off the bat. The first 100 pages, ending with his attendance at Dartmouth College, tend to drag sorely. Dad was a firefighter, Mom a secretary at a pencil manufacturer and housewife. Xgau's long reckoning with religious dogma, love for *Mad* magazine, baseball, and AM radio, first girlfriend Miriam, and enjoyment of jazz therewith are all touched upon (no pun intended), and along the way there are digressive treatises on the poetry of Samuel Taylor Coleridge and *Crime and Punishment* tossed in for good measure.

You should probably leave your snorkel on for the middle section, as the river of thick 1-9-6-0-s soup threatens to

Robert Christgau in New York City on October 17, 1978. Photo by Ebet Roberts/Redferns

drown everyone alive, then and now. This isn't all the writer's fault; to misappropriate Gertrude Stein, the '60s were the '60s were the '60s, and despite Christgau's obvious disdain for pablum ("Sixties nostalgia has been turning my stomach since approximately 1974"), he dutifully extolls on his attendance at heavy events: political gatherings of every stripe and persuasion, Woodstock, the Monterey Pop Festival, the 1968 Democratic National Convention in Chicago, and a lot of Rolling Stones concerts. Likewise, he reports on the ceaseless drift of politics, politics, and more politics.

Yet the finest sequences in *Going into the City* are those in which he discusses the meat-and-potatoes work of writing and editing some of the foundational texts of rock criticism, inside baseball about music publications large and small,

and his descriptions of writers he worked with and admired. Then again, color me obsessed. For a very long time, I've read about music with Greil Marcus, Lester Bangs, Richard Meltzer, and Ellen Willis perched on my shoulders like the fucking Four Horsemen of the Apocalypse. None of them were perfect, but the work of Marcus and Willis have aged best. Bangs and Meltzer got to me first and most profoundly; their messy screeds were written in my language, even as I recognize that they all too often wrote offensively about politics and race, and with appalling shallowness about women. As gender parity in rock criticism (all too slowly) improves, and the stature of Willis' work only seems to grow, my favorite pop critics—especially now—are far more adroit at expressing a quiet sort of self-doubt or at least political mindfulness than their

male forbears. This has not always been a specialty of criticism's (largely white) boys' club, or of Christgau himself. These days, even most white male critics would not see fit to call Jimi Hendrix a "psychedelic Uncle Tom" or craft a one-sentence review of a Donnas LP that simply reads "skank hos get fucked" even in jest. The Dean has done both.

As the book progresses, the litany of correspondents, associates, pals, writers he worked with, and kindred spirits he met on the basketball court and in art galleries and at political gatherings bleeds together in a Pynchon-esque rush that can be hard to follow, especially when he goes into thumbnail family or educational backgrounds on so many of these chums. Breaking down your most important friendships is one thing, but there are enough red-diaper babies outed over the course of this memoir to organize a Pampers factory. Christgau isn't a celebrity name-dropper, and he doesn't seem interested in hanging out with pop stars apart from a few very famous exceptions (would you be able to say no to John and Yoko?).

That's not to imply that Christgau doesn't dish. His dedication to laying out the myriad contours of his intellectual discourse, power struggles, and sexual relationships with women—most notably a few Sturm und Drang years in the late '60s with Ellen Willis (who passed away in 2006) and Carola Dibbell (his wife of over four decades and mother of their daughter)—yields mixed results. This is not because I think writing about the pleasures of boning is inherently corny or that the quest for reproduction and the joy of adoption is inherently beautiful; they just happen to be so in this book. Christgau treats the women in his life as fully flesh and blood, and maybe it's to his credit as a writer that they so often come off as much more interesting than he is. Far be it from me to judge his motives for such frankness, but as a dedicated Ellen Willis fan, I kept ping-ponging between wanting her side of the story—especially about what Christgau assures were many of their jointly arrived at theories of pop criticism—and a grim relief that she wasn't around to read certain portions of this book. His respect for her as a thinker, critic, and intellectual equal is impressive, and his heartbreak over the end of their love affair is palpable indeed, but we could've easily been spared his description of her breasts, or his obvious remorse at having had sex with her on the same day she was raped by an intruder in their stairwell.

My sense of NYC geography isn't sharp, but it strikes me that Christgau has spent much of his life living within 10 square miles. That, and the professional project of his life—listening to records 8 to 12 hours a day and writing 15,000 record reviews over an almost 50-year career—is a monument to insane focus. Although reading this book left me feeling even more strongly that the project is worth celebrating, I don't feel especially connected to its author. That doesn't mean the man can't write up a storm. A lovely section of the book details the creation of one of his finest works, "In Memory of the Dave Clark Five," in 1969. The piece is a travelogue mostly about listening to the radio in a car—it barely mentions the DC5 and has a lot of not-so-thinly-veiled #realtalk about his heartbreak over Willis, but it somehow doesn't lean too hard on sentiment or rock criticism or anything much at all, apart from how music simply makes you feel more alive. Like the 5th Dimension song he describes, music is "not quite real, but it's far from false, and that is very sad and very beautiful. Like most things, if you're in the mood."

Most rock critics could reasonably expect a party and a cake for their 60th birthday, but in 2002, the Dean's current and former coworkers wrote him a book. In celebration, a few dozen of the many writers he has championed contributed essays to a privately published collection printed and bound by Nortex Press in Austin, Texas, entitled *Don't Stop 'Til You Get Enough: Essays in Honor of Robert Christgau*. When it came out, I eagerly bought a copy. Like this memoir, I had hoped that it would solve a personal mystery: Why has his work been so essential to rock criticism, yet left me so utterly cold? The book's contributors were of unimpeachable quality: Ann Powers, Rob Sheffield, Dave Hickey, Gary Giddins, Holly George-Warren, Greil Marcus, Simon Frith, Greg Tate. Accolades to his writing style competed with tales of hot, hard-fought line edits at the editor's apartment with the editor himself barely clothed (it's bedrock Xgau myth that he has edited male writers in the nude, although he disputes it), and what-if fantasias about his own missed-out-upon "rock star" career—a sweet honorarium from an impressive flock of writers he helped bring to the fold. But as I finished it, I was no closer to breaking the ice. Twelve years later, after reading a congratulatory memoir the man has just penned about himself, I'm still not.

The *Village Voice* fired Christgau in 2006. Financial troubles and cutbacks at the paper had cut down the champion of the music consumer and curator of the famed annual Pazz & Jop critics' poll in the venue where he'd done his most famous work. Like his career at the country's premier alt-weekly, a top-down chapter of homogeny in rock criticism's history seemed to be closing for good. Flung to the winds like so many others, the Dean of American Rock Critics contributes to *Billboard*, writes his Consumer Guide for medium.com, teaches at NYU, and maintains his massive archival website. But the beat—and with it, the search for newer voices and other rooms—goes on.

READING LIST

Going into the City: Portrait of the Critic as a Young Man
by Robert Christgau
(2015 Harper Collins)

**VINYL GEMS IN THE
CUTOUT BIN**
BY SCOTT SEWARD

Mime Rock

Band: Hello People

Album: Bricks

Label: ABC, 1975

We begin with epic understatement: Mimes are a hard sell in the 21st century. They have—along with circus clowns, politicians, and Kris Jenner—become the most hated and feared citizens on earth. Despite the fact that they are in no way as ubiquitous as they were in the mime- and clown-crazy 1970s, when they littered city sidewalks like pre-pooper-scooper-law dog doo, not hating mimes in 2015 means risking public shame and ridicule. By the turn of the '80s, oversized rainbow suspenders were the only legacy left by these practitioners of the infernal Gallic art of mimography. (Mimery? Whatever.)

The Hello People—mime/musicians who were taught how to work their way out of invisible boxes by a French master who shall remain nameless out of respect for his heirs—gained a modicum of fame during the '60s by turning out wilted-flower power pop that made sunny acts like the Association and the Sandpipers sound like gritty poets of the barrio. The Smothers Brothers were big fans.

You would have thought that the ironic gimmick of singing mimes would have lasted for about a minute, but *somehow*—and we will never know exactly how because people are too embarrassed to ask him—prog rock and pop's busiest beaver, Todd Rundgren, hooked up with the Hello People and made two fine albums with the group. He toured with them off and on for years and even had them mime onstage for him at times, for chrissakes. Vietnam did strange things to this nation.

The first Todd-produced album, 1974's *The Handsome Devils*, is excellent, supremely stoned acid rock and pop— highly recommended to anyone interested in Todd Rundgren or dubbed-out '70s studio hijinks. The cover, however, is a terrifying photo of a pissed-off, screaming, afroed glam-mime with flexed tongue frenulum. It's a nightmare-inducing shot, so we'll move on to 1975's completely enjoyable *Bricks* instead. *Bricks* does have

some dross. It's an "updated" take on '50s nugget "Book of Love," for one, and thus a double whammy of '70s fetish objects: annoying street performers and the doo-wop era. There is a trademark Todd Rundgren ballad, "It Wouldn't Have Made Any Difference," that is dressed for senior prom success, but that falls short. There is another track that sounds and smells exactly like Little Feat if that band had been replaced by mime robots.

The first stunner on *Bricks* is the slow-moving "Dinosaur." See, 1975 was a year when combining disco, glam, and '60s acid rock guitar provided untold riches—and then Johnny Rotten came along and ruined everything. "Mad Red Ant Lady" is the next keeper. Goofy, for sure, but in a way that is endearing rather than being a Frank Zappa puritanical booby joke. Plus, there is lots of screaming. The instrumental "Faces" is worth the 50 cents this album will cost you all by itself; the just-funky-enough disco rhythm combined with a plethora of bouncing synth sounds *and* languid guitar solos *and* the extended drum break filled with cat and bird imitations in the background *and* the faux–Native American war cries *and* the screaming make this a perfect candidate for your new personal theme song. In general, Todd Rundgren's dork majik works wonders on the guitars throughout the album, and for all I know he played everything while his silent pals stood there like living statues. Perhaps Todd had a mime shadow-self within that could only find expression via proximity to these four anonymous grease-painted nudniks. We all have our demons.

A Psycho-Culinary Analysis of Joe Walsh's *But Seriously, Folks*

One of the first psychological inklings of fatherhood (besides suddenly desiring to order a beret from the *New Yorker*) is that the late-period musical catalogue of Joe Walsh inexplicably emerges from itself the way a snake emerges from its own skin—suddenly becoming slick, dangerous, and new.

If you are a dad, you have probably already come to the same conclusions that I have about Joe Walsh. You understand, for example, that the James Gang is irreproachable in the same way that Cream is, and that it was one of the greatest stripped-down, straight-ahead rock-and-roll bands of all time and generally too hot to last. It didn't last, specifically, because Joe Walsh got called up by the Eagles, who were tired of Bernie Leadon and his tinkling banjo and needed Walsh to play the hypnotized guitar solo on "Hotel California" and otherwise rescue them from becoming a disco band. It's also fairly well understood that the effect of hitting the jackpot and replacing Leadon in the Eagles was psychologically traumatic for Walsh.

Besides expressing his hang-ups in a legendary pattern of hotel-room destruction, drug abuse, and hijinks with such like-minded co-conspirators as Keith Moon and John Belushi, Walsh also wrote and recorded a magnificent solo album during the period when he was joining the Eagles: *But Seriously, Folks*. The album's crown jewel, "Life's Been Good to Me So Far," is, of course, a barely veiled recognition of the guilt Walsh felt about suddenly finding himself filthy rich. The song vibrates uncomfortably against another of the album's great tunes, "Second Hand Store," which opens with the self-explanatory line, "You lost your color when you painted the town." Which is to say that the album wears its heart on its sleeve to the same raw degree that the first Plastic Ono Band album does—albeit on completely different terms. As the first line of *But Seriously, Folks* proclaims, "I'm out in the open, easy to see...like keeping a secret everyone knows."

Heart on its sleeve or not, no one has yet, to my knowledge, performed a serious psychoanalysis of the album cover of *But Seriously, Folks*, which features a photograph of Joe Walsh floating at a bistro table within a swimming pool in front of plate of lobster and bagels and various other food items. Certainly no one has yet performed a culinary psychoanalysis of the album cover culminating in a dynamite recipe for psychologically significant lobster rolls.

Naturally, the best antidote to psychological suffering is to materialize the symbols and metaphors that comprise one's neuroses as ingredients for a delicious sandwich, and then to hungrily eat that sandwich. With that in mind, here is an itemized recipe constructed from the psychologically important elements on the album cover of Joe Walsh's *But Seriously, Folks*.

TIP

A lobster is a classic and
perplexing Jungian symbol.

The Swimming Pool Referring to the general scarcity of—and therefore obsession with—water in the West, Joan Didion noticed, "The symbolic content of swimming pools has always been interesting: a pool is misapprehended as a trapping of affluence, real or pretended, and of a kind of hedonistic attention to the body. Actually a pool is, for many of us in the West, a symbol not of affluence but of order, of control over the uncontrollable." Certainly the image of Walsh submerged in a swimming pool can be comfortably translated as "drowning in affluence" or, as Didion recommends, "illusory psychological control." More interestingly, the swimming pool refers to the Jungian alchemical image of a king drowning in water or, more contemporaneously, the image of Dustin Hoffman floating in the swimming pool in *The Graduate*, paralyzed by the water against confronting his future.

The Lobster A lobster is a classic and perplexing Jungian symbol, expressing our deep fear of the dark and the paralyzing world of the sea. The lobster is also a pure analogue of the "alien" or "dinosaur" archetype: as alive and sentient as we are, yet confrontationally foreign and weird. The lobster is also, of course, powerfully suggestive of affluence and carefree country-club life and so calls from "the ocean" of the subconscious various tinges of guilt, inadequacy, and covetousness. The powerfulness of the lobster for Joe Walsh requires no explanation.

The Bagels, the Tablecloth, the Lemon, and the Head of Lettuce Joe Walsh grew up in New York and New Jersey (home of the bagel and the Italian checkered tablecloth) but was transplanted to Los Angeles (home of the lemon and the salad) in order to join the Eagles. Robert Christgau famously described the Eagles as "suave and synthetic—brilliant, but false." The same could be said of the city of Los Angeles. Walsh surely looked upon his adopted landscape with the forever-nagging discomfort of an outsider.

The Beer Sometimes a beer is just a beer.

The Corn Joe Walsh was born in Wichita, Kansas, which sits within a fathomless sea of cornfields. The cob of corn is psychologically significant insofar as the circumstances of our births are always psychologically significant.

The Salt And The Pepper These particular salt and pepper shakers have what appear to be small wilting potted datura plants painted on them. Datura plants are notoriously poisonous and are psychologically associated with Victorian murder plots and melancholia.

The Mayonnaise It is more or less impossible to construct a lobster roll without mayonnaise, so we will *assume* there is some mayonnaise in that sugar bowl.

Lobster Rolls à la Walsh

INGREDIENTS for 2 LOBSTER ROLLS

1 TBS WATER: add as needed to thin lobster salad

1 WHOLE LOBSTER: boiled, cooled, and picked

2 BAGELS: lightly toasted, sliced in half

½ HEAD BUTTER LETTUCE: finely chopped

½ LEMON: juiced

1 BEER: served cold alongside lobster roll

SALT AND PEPPER: to taste

½ CUP MAYONNAISE

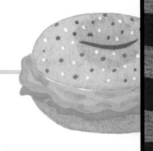

INSTRUCTIONS

Bring a large pot of water to boil.

Add the whole lobster and cook for 12 to 15 minutes.

Remove lobster and let cool until it can be comfortably handled.

Pick the claw and tail meat.

Blend in a bowl with the mayonnaise, lemon juice, and corn kernels.

Add salt and pepper.

Add water, as needed, to thin the salad.

Slice the bagels in half and lightly toast.

Finely chop the butter lettuce.

To construct the lobster roll, heap a mound of salad onto one bagel half.

Add the chopped lettuce and the other half of the bagel.

Serve with a cold glass of beer. Enjoy!

PITCHFORK TOONS

SPRING 2015

NOT FREE!

.TOONS

FOR THOSE OF US WHO LOVE TO READ BUT MAYBE NOT ALL THE TIME

WORD & PANEL

The WTF of Comics

ODY-C (Matt Fraction)

THIS QUARTER IN *TOONS*!

① **Zak Sally**
② **Sara Lautman**
③ **Tim Lahan**

Genre-splicing, hairpin plot turns, characters losing their minds and finding them again, talking plantlife, scenarios that beggar belief—movies and TV still can't come close, no matter how many superhero flicks get cranked out.

As those superhero flicks began to generate profits in the nine figures, too many genre comics seemed more and more like movie and TV pitches (hello, Mark Millar). Comics invaded TV (*The Walking Dead*, *The Flash*, *Gotham*) and movies (just look at any multiplex), and genre comics went into a long period of just being more middlebrow crap. Grant Morrison once said that too many comics in the 21st century had a "within budget" feeling about them. BINGO.

Yet who can blame the artists and writers? Comics have always been a terrible way to make a living. Writing comics is incredibly hard work and the money is lousy. The profits from movies and TV runs laps around that of comics.

Still, there are certainly signs of life, especially from Image Comics. Brian K. Vaughan and Fiona Staples' science-fantasy comic *Saga* (Image) does this perfectly. It's smart, feminist, character-driven, and would look completely absurd on film. (There's a whole host of bad guys who have TVs for heads, including a janitor with an old black-and-white tube model, and a fat king with an enormous flat-screen). Vaughan has worked in the TV industry, and it's clear that he and Staples know exactly what they're doing—*Saga* is pure comics madness.

Comics creators Matt Fraction and Kelly Sue DeConnick are a married couple. Both have done their share of superhero books and *manga* translations. But Fraction's *ODY-C* is just what I'm talking about: an all-female space-opera retelling of The Odyssey that looks like it came straight out of a French absinthe dream. DeConnick's *Bitch Planet* is a sci-fi feminist riff on women-in-prison flicks, where women are jailed for "non-compliance." These are stories that wouldn't work in any other medium.

As comic book properties continue to migrate to the screen, comics have to continually strive to push harder and be stranger. I want comics doing stuff that would look idiotic on screen, that would make audiences go "Oh come on." I want to see the infinite special-effects budget that drawing on a page allows. I want to go from Atlantis 50,000 years ago to 4535 A.D. on a terraformed Mars in the space of a single panel. I want comics to stretch and bend time from page to page. I want red herrings and coincidences that would embarrass the cast of *Scandal*.

I want to mumble "WTF?" with every plot twist and page turn. I want comics to go to there, to set up shop there, to give us things we absolutely, positively cannot get anywhere else.

→ *JOE GROSS*

Zak Sally would like it known that a Low cover of "Little Drummer Boy" (from their self-released *Christmas EP*) was used in a Christmas campaign for The Gap during his tenure in the band, with his full compliance. He'd be happy to talk about how, why, and how that happened, with anyone who asks.

* EVEN IF IT'S SOME KIND OF "COOL" "LIFESTYLE"... jesus, it's *repulsive*.

What the Fuck Did He Say? On Young Thug and the Abstraction of Rap

BY BRIAN ZARLEY

ILLUSTRATIONS BY JEFFERSON CHENG

At long last! Here is something with which we can knit together, with those big ugly centipede stitches, both the old-school, dyed-in-the-wool, realer-than-real, best bring your thesaurus rap Brahmins and the young blossoms of the populist, laptop, sound cloud, smoke cloud, BlackWhiteGayAsianFemaleFullSexualIdentitySpectrum narcissus bloom flowering in the sticky patina of the blood of the music industry era: Neither one seems to have any clue what the fuck, exactly, Young Thug is saying, and at least a few of them are pretty damned upset about it. Blessed union! It is time to put aside those vast, sweeping differences with which the Brahmins and blossoms build their respective taxonomies of rap, and unite against one artist who pushes—not singularly, but certainly harder and louder—against the few vast, sweeping similarities which constitute the most basic structures of the genre. Seriously, is Young Thug even rapping?

Thugga at his best, when he is at his most inscrutable and idiosyncratic, frightfully singular, does not rap on the track, or within it. He is not riding the beat, or breathing in the spaces between it, but seems to take flight above it, erratic, lepidopteran, voltaic, all serrated gulps, strangled whelps, flagellated moans; he sounds like a neon cat o' nine tails scoring the night sky or acid in the Bellagio fountain, like high speed ballistic footage of chameleon tongues blown out and over saturated and stained with crystal violet. There are dizzying climbs, peregrine dives, burt-fire assaults, spiraling Catherine wheels, and if all this sounds like desperately reaching, synesthetic stabs at something impossible to describe, that's exactly the point; what Young Thug is doing, when he hits escape velocity and leaves our generally accepted descriptors and definitions behind, is pushing rap, as all art forms are inevitably pushed, towards its bleeding, ragged edge, dissolving strictures and structures and moving beyond the inherent limitations of representational, even expressional art, slowly pushing towards the holy summit of abstraction.

What so frustrated Alex Williams and caused the admittedly Herculean satirical effort of Aaerios Gaming Channel is the hyper-realized, anonymity-accentuated equivalent of the sneering museum goer who sucks their teeth at Jackson Pollock or earnestly believes themselves capable of painting a Mark Rothko. The abstraction of art, be it elegant or brutal, adroit or gauche, is above all liberating; it is a requisite rebellion from the heavy onus to make something resemble something else, and while music has never found itself beholden to mimesis—

indeed, aside from some aural bunting and a few bookends, representational sounds, e.g. crickets or rain or thunder or traffic or cloying imitations thereof, are mostly non grata in popular music—that does not mean it is free from constrictions; if anything, it is just the opposite, as fans and bloggers and critics and theorists and recording artists commingle in various spheres—sometimes in real time—to pass judgment, coin genres, listen for parsing or pleasure and all the while constructing a byzantine consensus for what various kinds of music are and are not. Think of the million subtle shades, to the initiated, of metal, or the nuances hidden in the sybaritic throbbing of the sundry forms of electronic dance music driving ilium on a million different gloaming dance floors, and realize the incredible complexity—and potential for garroting—in the cat's cradle we've built.

Rap is certainly not free from its own hounding catalogue of conventions; while there are many kinds of rap music, and even more styles of rapping, there are a few comfortably standard (or as standard as possible when one is talking about the entire breadth of musical consideration tout le monde) components with which we listen to, and stratify, rappers: flow—which, in this essay, consists of rhythm and rhyme—delivery, lyrical content, rhetorical dexterity. While the most narrow definition of rapping is rhythmic speech over a beat, this was abandoned relatively early, with rappers incorporating singsongy hooks and affectations before the eventual rise of melodic sing-rapping, e.g. Bone Thugs-n-Harmony (and its inverse, rap-singing, most notably practiced by R. Kelly), and the emergence of rappers who are also capable singers, injecting a healthy dose of R&B into the oeuvre.

While any number of rappers regularly push against the boundaries of what we consider rapping to be, none—or at least none with comparable mainstream success and credibility—push as hard as Young Thug. In abandoning not only the stereotypic deliveries and flows of his peers, but also fearlessly jettisoning the most sacrosanct and base of rap's elements—there are none who treat lyrics as thrillingly cavalier—Thugga is at the forefront of the abstraction of rap.

What a horrid constriction, a dumb oppression, to require art to resemble something real! Look you, scoffing at those huge fuzzy vibrating unnerving (somehow, and that's the real nut of it) colored rectangles

"

He is not riding the beat, or breathing in the spaces between it, but seems to take flight above it, erratic, lepidopteran, voltaic, all serrated gulps, strangled whelps, flagellated moans; he sounds like a neon cat o' nine tails scoring the night sky or acid in the Bellagio fountain.

"

BRIAN ZARLEY

of Mark Rothko's, it took a long time to reach the point of human expression wherein we could conceptualize such a seemingly simple thing. For most of human history, the ever-flowing font of our creativity—for the visual arts, in particular, which run neck and neck with literature as our "highest" form—was whipsawed by stenotic gatekeepers who required both mimesis and morality; make your thing look like what is, and speak to our souls—no, preach—to boot! To do anything else would be to waste your time, God's time, and our own, and so long as time was a precious resource (i.e., for most of recorded history until our latest eyelash-thin slice) the stenotic minority, in conjunction, of course, with the artists themselves and the larger milieu, insisted upon representational, high quality, moral art being the only art.

To arrive at Abstract Expressionism is to come up hard against the edge of visual art and be greeted with the strange abyssal denizens that lay beyond it. The process was long and convoluted, but there are seminal moments easy to identify; James Abbot McNeil Whistler's before the bar defense of his *Nocturne in Black and Gold: The Falling Rocket* from the vicious mauling of king pearl-clutcher and art critic John Ruskin, for example, which helped birth the Aesthetic movement summed up thusly, by Algernon Charles Swinburne, as being for "Art for art's sake, first of all," a heretical notion indeed. Other late 19th century movements, most notably Expressionism, put an emphasis on humanity's inner workings, as opposed to mirroring its everyday. Expressionism, according to *Oxford Art Online*, "should be understood as a form of 'new Humanism,' which sought to communicate man's spiritual life." To the Impressionist's disdain for the chitinous processes of didactic painting, the Expressionists added contempt for focus upon the concrete.

The early 20th century, afflicted by cruelties and horrors unlike any that had come before it, seemed to shatter the collective consciousness of visual art; here we find Dada, wherein subversive absurdity expressed the artist's abhorrence for their current climate. Mimesis and realism was cast to the wayside; who would want to resemble, even tacitly, a world which had birthed the Great War? From the short-lived but massively influential Dada movement (see: Duchamp's famous urinal and the questions it raises about art and us) came the Surrealists, whose fever-dream practices sought to replicate, in real life, the unconscious, which they held—in conjunction with the exciting works of Freud—may have an even greater impact on reality than the waking life. Here, finally,

spring to life shapes and forms which have no analogue. Turning the Surrealists' inward facing loupe on art itself were the Dutch practitioners being espoused in De Stijil ("the style"), neo-plasticists including Piet Mondrian, who championed expression through abstraction.

"As a pure representation of the human mind, art will express itself in an aesthetically purified, that is to say, abstract form," Mondrian wrote in the essay "Neo-Plasticism in Pictorial Art." Mondrian believed that his "new plastic idea" could not therefore be expressed in representation, but in the very principles which comprise it, color and line. Lifted of their burden to form something which our eyes and minds can easily recognize, color and line become free to challenge larger, intangible aspects of existence, a crucial revelation (as Surrealism and other styles of art were before it) to creatures for whom the inner life is as important, if not more so, than the outer. What the Abstract Expressionists we are most familiar with—de Kooning, Pollock, Twombly, Rothko—did was to apply the purity of Mondrian's new plastic idea with the spiritual urges contained in Vassily Kandinsky's extremely influential essay, "On the Spiritual in Art," wherein some of the earliest ideals of abstraction were laid, to utilize abstraction to in an attempt to portray the panoply of human existence which we feel and experience, rather than simply see.

Kandinsky envied music's inherent tilt towards capturing the spiritual via abstraction. Music, according to On the Spiritual in Art, "achieves results which are beyond the realm of painting" when it comes to certain forms of internal expression, as it, "by its very nature, is ultimately and fully emancipated and needs no outer form for its expression." One can, after all, write a love song which never once mentions love, or portend certain ominous doom via pure aural structure, forms of abstraction with which we are seemingly naturally attuned. What Young Thug is doing, however, holds just as much in common with abstraction in the painterly sense as it does the intrinsically musical; the parallels are not perfect (dancing about architecture and all), but in sloughing off one of the key components of rap, his oddest verses find kindred spirits in the anguished drippings of Pollock or the intricate cloudy assaults of Kandinsky.

Certain tenants of rap music have been thoroughly broken before [consider how Rick Ross's continued

> "This point has not been reached, but if and when it is, the entire idea of rapping will be put to an existential test, and it will almost certainly be because of Young Thug.

commercial, critical, and peer acceptance—despite his outing as a former corrections officer—has effectively eliminated the dread onus of Being Real.] The eccentricities of Kool Keith applied the language of rap to subject matter not contained by any one corner or street or city or planet. With rap music now among our most populist forms of expression—all one needs is a decent microphone, a laptop, and a closet to release a mixtape—these stylistic departures are coming fast and furious. It is not difficult to hear a hint of Dada in Riff Raff's "Teriyaki suit with the lemon Phantom/ Heavyweight heartburn: Mylanta," or to envision Tristan Tzara tip-toeing with the leaned out preying mantis. In songs of cocaine and ostentation, Ross—as fine an actor as any—can actually be heard speaking to the savage desire which fuels our nation's anomic impulse for success, particularly success not only earned but taken, taken from the institutional and societal evils which can stack odds high enough to blot out the sun, obliquely referencing the socioeconomic and racial politics which were a foundational element of hip-hop with a stylization as heavy as the message.

Recording artists like Chance the Rapper or Kendrick Lamar often twist, torque, elasticize, or similarly distort their lyrics and flows (eg. Kendrick telling her what she wants on "Fuckin' Problems"), but few embrace it so recklessly, or imbue it with as much passion, as Young Thug, which is why he is at the forefront of the abstraction of rap.

A brief, yet critical, caveat: Let us make it perfectly clear that, in freeing himself from holy commitment to lyricism, Thugga's words by no means mean nothing. While not the most nimble of rappers, it would be foolish—and more than a bit regressive—to say that he is not saying anything; quite the contrary, as his liquid aspects of masculinity and unique twist on the common rap tropes—not meant as a pejorative—make a close listen to his bars a rewarding experience. It is because this is not necessary for a rewarding experience that Young Thug is unique; it is because one does not even necessarily have to comprehend his lyrics for a rewarding experience that he is revolutionary.

Of the major components by which we we judge and listen to rap, most rappers lean upon—and are thereby understood in relationship to—some combination of flow and lyricism; we are considering, with varying weights, their lyrics and how they are structured, as well as what they are saying. This is relatively analogous to representational art, insomuch as metaphor, synecdoche, and other rhetorical skills, while not slavishly descriptive, form concrete associations in our head. The abstraction comes from Young Thug's emphasis on delivery, how the verses are presented to us; the emotional weight in his bars no longer lays primarily with what the words say, but in how he is saying them.

BRIAN ZARLEY

Listening to "Stoner" or "Danny Glover" is akin to standing before Cy Twombly's *The First Part of the Return to Parnassus,* wherein some recognizable figures—crude pictographs, really—surface for us as anchors, safe places amidst an angry whorl, like the time–lapse of a hurricane's path, of blood and ash.

Thugga's push into abstraction seems purposeful; in going from the *I Came From Nothing* series, wherein Thug's style is to mixtape-era Lil Wayne as early Action Bronson's was to Ghostface Killah, to *1017 Thug* and on to the abrasively, gloriously stylized flows of *Black Portland,* Young Thugga *Mane La Flare,* and his work with Rich Gang, artistic intent is obvious. The *I Came From Nothing* tape, while mostly straight-ahead in its bars, contains, in its warbling hooks and croaking addendums—the outros

on "Spartan" and "Ball on Y'all" come to mind—the first vestiges of what will come to be Young Thug's signature style. In listening through for some kind of key conceptual moment, his screaming ascendence, on the back end of *1017 Thug*'s "Scared of Ya," into his singular melodic mode seems especially important; by "Nigeria," one track later, the entire song finds Thugga rapping in the manner which inspired this essay's introductory salvos.

To listen from "Nigeria" onward is to be pushed, with

alarming celerity, into Thugga's brave new world, one held aloft by his most popular songs: "Stoner," "Danny Glover," "Lifestyle." Listening to "Stoner" or "Danny Glover" is akin to standing before Cy Twombly's *The First Part of the Return to Parnassus*, wherein some recognizable figures, crude pictographs, really, surface for us as anchors, safe places, amidst an angry whorl—like the time-lapse of a hurricane's path—of blood and ash; we can hear Thugga, can place words—including high fashion brands, those obvious icons of success, and expletives—and ideas, but are overwhelmed by his sheer expression. It is not without reason that, following the soft, gentle bridge (even here, the most recognizable word—"Dabo"—is deviously esoteric), Thugga explodes into a staccato assault, shattering the stoned out peace like gunshots on a summer night.

It is in his insistence on challenging us, not only with lyrics but also—more so—with how they are delivered, that Young Thug is most indispensable. The infectious, approachable bounce of a DJ Mustard beat, a sound currently saturating popular radio, is rendered completely alien in *The Purple Album*'s "Riding Around" via Thugga's insistence on distorting, to the point of incomprehensibility, the most familiar and friendly aspect of a song, the hook. In combination with his comparatively tame verse, it becomes difficult not to see "Riding Around"'s hook as a subversive gesture; you will sing along, because it remains catchy as fuck, but damn if you will not sound as if under general anesthesia, your lips rapidly cycling through amoebic shapes unrelated to the English alphabet, whilst doing so.

The accessibility of the song and Young Thug's verses upon it share an inverse relationship. Take "Lifestyle:" a slick, perfectly constructed song, lacquered perfectly with an early-aughts dirty South candy-paint shine and featuring noted stylists Birdman (in a glorified, but glorious, cameo) and Rich Homie Quan. The single most challenging aspect of "Lifestyle," what keeps it from potentially becoming quick-hit aspartame, is Young Thug's voice. Thug assails the radio ready song both lyrically—why invoke Quan, in homage, by declaring "Quan voice!" rather than mimic him? This is a blatant abstraction of the semi-common rapper's tool mimicry (albeit an ironic one, as it makes crystal clear his intentions), calling attention to the formation and implementation of a rap lyric, the delivery, more so than what it is saying—and via delivery per se. Even if one does not comprehend, at first listen, what he is literally saying, Thugga's delivery alone contains the pained straining and ebullient, lofting victory that are at the heart of the song; this is Abstract Expressionism in spirit, if not form (there are, after all, real words in there, even if you cannot hear them initially). The full-out abstraction of rap would sound something like Black Moth Super Rainbow's singing, completely devoid of any recognizable utterances with which to save and orient ourselves. This point has not been reached, but when or if it is, the entire idea of rapping will be put to an existential test—almost certainly by Young Thug.

Young Thug is pioneering—sometimes painfully, sometimes masterfully, always arrestingly—a new form of expression for the rapper, one wherein lyrics can serve as a vehicle for delivery (which in turn is a vessel for emotions and ideas) rather than the opposite. The best rappers can dominate a track, pin it and us down and spit, flow, shackle us with their words; think the righteous fury of Kanye West, ejaculating on expensive furs, or the hyper-real, detail driven stories of Ghostface, whose "Shakey Dog" is a short film as much as it is a rap song. Compare this to Young Thug's turn on "Givenchy," wherein his domination is more like that of a guitar solo's, an atavistic conquest first realized through sound and scope and only later with lyrical content. Thugga's "Givenchy" is aching and aspirational, violent and beautiful, and it is all these things before one even takes the time to hear his words; few, if any, recording artists could claim a similar expressive mode, which lays close to the Abstract Expressionist's. That delivery is the primary impetus behind a Young Thug verse is to put to the forefront the emotional aspect of rap, a raw engagement impossible for even the most eloquent of backpackers. As he dissolves, he does so into something that manages to be at various times druggy and desperate, hungry and dangerous, triumphant and sharp, helter-skelter and sexual. He is motion and color on the cut.

What exactly Young Thug is saying is this: Rap's Cambrian Explosion has accelerated an already rapidly evolving medium. Already artists of various ethnicities and ethoses have left behind the old standards, our past deliminations of who is and is not a rapper seeming more narrow—and foolish—by the day, and as we have expanded our definitions of who a rapper is, so too must we question what rapping is. A staid form is a dead one, and Young Thug is racing forward; what he is saying—expressing—is life. ✐

BRIAN ZARLEY *is a critic living in Chicago.*

How to Raise Hell in Three Steps

On Run–D.M.C., Parliament, Blackness & Revolution

BY CARVELL WALLACE

1

In 1987, in a small southwestern Pennsylvania steel town, I was the only black kid I knew.

I was also the only kid with a copy of Run-D.M.C.'s *Raising Hell*. At the time those two facts seemed to be very much connected.

For those who haven't had the pleasure, being the only black kid in middle school is a little like having a disease that you don't want to talk about and don't want anyone else to talk about either. You feel ashamed. You feel guilty. When you get to the three or four paragraphs in your social studies book about slavery, you try to look so deeply engrossed in taking notes that you don't even notice how many kids are stealing glances at you. And you don't even take notes.

You feel like black is hateful. You feel like black makes people uncomfortable and unhappy. You feel like black is your fault. Because you are a kid.

So this weird thing happened with the Run-D.M.C. tape-Whenever I made copies of it for white kids whose parents wouldn't let them have it, I always left off this one song:

It was called "Proud to Be Black":

> *I'm proud to be black, y'all*
> *And that's a fact, y'all*
> *And if you try to take what's mine, I'll take it back, y'all*
> *It's like that.*

That song bothered the ever-loving shit out of me. The thought of the white kids I went to school with listening to it made me cringe. Why did I have to have a song that made it OK to be who I was? Why did I have to be so lame, and so ridiculous, that Run-D.M.C. needed to devote the weakest, corniest track on an album full of bangers just to making me feel special? The problem wasn't that I was black. The problem was that black was something so terrible that it needed a hip-hop PSA just to be alright. That was some embarrassing shit for an 11-year-old.

None of the white kids I knew needed that.

I didn't want to need that. So I just ignored the song entirely.

In a seemingly unrelated story, there was this one kid named Jason who liked to call me a nigger. A lot. Nigger this. Nigger that. How many niggers does it take. Did you hear about the nigger who. Hey nigger. Shut up nigger.

I wasn't much of a fighter. I was more of a book reader and clarinet practicer. But Jason made me angry. More than angry. He made me seethe. That's the word you use when you hate something so very deeply, but you feel that forces bigger than you are preventing you from doing anything about it.

Seethe.

One day, this other kid who I wasn't even really friends with took pity on me and offered the following advice:

"You oughta just fuckin' punch him in the face."

"Really?"

"Just… fuckin'… sucker-punch him, dude."

"You think so?"

"Fuck yeah, dude. I wouldn't let him talk to me like that if I was you."

I guess that was all I needed to hear because 20 minutes later, when Jason walked past me, I hit him directly in the mouth as hard as I could. I wanted to draw blood. I wanted to knock him unconscious. I wanted to kill him. I wanted him to never be able to say the word "nigger" again.

But all that happened was I got his spit on my knuckles, which were now sore. It was intense and kind of gross.

He looked at me with something I can only describe as bewilderment.

"What the hell was that for?"

I shrugged.

"You know what it was for."

He never bothered me again.

Even still. I fast forwarded past that stupid Run-D.M.C. song every fucking time it came on.

2

Four years later, I bought my first Parliament record at a store on the corner of Hollywood and Highland. I had since left Small Town America and moved to L.A. to live with my mother.

It was, you could say, a jarring transition. Hollywood was a was a different kind of place then. It was seedy and uncomfortable, piss-smelling and prostitute-y. Grimy. The intersection of Hollywood and Highland in the '90s had a deep sense of failure.

It was on this corner that I listened to *The Clones of Dr. Funkenstein* for the first time. I don't know why I chose that one; it was completely random. I was afraid to ask for help. I had been told Parliament was good. I grabbed the first one in the section, paid for it, walked out, put it in my Walkman, and hit play.

What I heard next literally made no sense. Weird, sped-up voices. Galactic Pyramids. Gross sexual metaphors. Non-sensical lyrics. Unnecessary use of multisyllabic words. It was uncomfortably sick. Ludicrous and nonsensical lyrically, but surgically, almost magically proficient musically. The combination was downright creepy.

Standing there listening to it was kind of nice. I didn't feel like getting back on the bus to Van Nuys. I didn't feel like going anywhere at all. So, I stayed. I didn't move from that corner until both sides had played. I bummed a cigarette. I watched cops arrest a dude who was yelling. I saw about four near auto accidents. I smelled weed. I peed in an alley between two buildings.

I had just turned 15 years old.

Something else happened that day. I realized that I really liked being an anonymous kid on a street corner in L.A. I realized that I really liked not giving a solitary fuck about what anyone was doing, not even myself. I realized that in some way it was my natural state.

Two days later, I started dressing differently.

I cut my own hair into a weird nappy mushroom top. I took this goofy trench coat I had and sliced it at the waist with a pair of scissors. On the chest I sewed the patch that I earned in a middle school spelling bee. I wrote graffiti on the sleeve in Sharpie. I took to wearing pajama bottoms and black chucks.

In short, the combination of Parliament and Hollywood had instantly funked me out.

And it worked, because the first time I left the house in this new uniform, I experienced something that I never had before. You might call it freedom. Abandon. Cultural immunity. I had a self. It was adolescent and awkward and trying too hard. But it was my very own self. It was a me that was all mine. It didn't matter what anyone thought about it. For a brief moment in time, I simply didn't give a fuck.

And that's an important thing. When you have come to regard your very skin color as an insufferable disease, when you have to punch other people in the mouth just so you can be OK with who you are, not giving a fuck is the single most divine experience you can ever have.

3

On that very same corner twenty years later, the LAPD killed a man who was wielding a Swiss Army knife. He was a street performer. His schtick was dressing up as the *Scream* dude and freaking out tourists before posing with them for photos. Police were responding to a report of a stabbing. They arrived, saw the man, and he apparently approached them.

In 2014, we learned that this could mean anything. Did he turn toward them when they called out? Did he start toward them to explain that he was a performer? Did he turn into a superhuman and run through fire and bullets while tearing his shirt off? We don't know. All we know is that he had a Swiss Army knife, and a group of trained officers felt that their lives were in danger. So, as an LAPD spokeswoman put it in the noncommittal cop speak to which we've all become woefully accustomed, "an officer-involved shooting occurred."

That word. Occurred. Like rain occurs. Or wind. An officer-involved shooting is an act of nature that happens of its own volition.

The stab victim was never located.

It's been a really shitty year for stuff like this.

Mike Brown's shooting occurred, Tamir Rice's shooting occurred, Eric Garner's death by asphyxiation occurred. Jordan Crawford's shooting in a Wal-Mart occurred. A whole lot of death at the hands of police has occurred.

Black folks have realized, en masse, that we have to start fighting all over again. For the umpteenth fucking time. We had hoped we were done. Or at least done enough to have a life that doesn't involve taking to the streets in order to be considered human. Apparently we were wrong. Even white people have started to wonder if maybe the racist system is unfair in a way that should actually matter to them.

People have gathered in protest. Thought pieces have been fired off. Tweets have scored in the 10-thousands on favorites. Comedians have been serious. Riot gear has been donned. Windows broken. Fires set.

The victims are all still dead. The killers are still free.

So what now.

As a general rule, no one really wants a revolution. They are a lot of work and are tremendously inconvenient. Especially in this country. We have a lot to relax over. I'm writing this on a comfortable chair in a decent home. You are very likely reading this on a device the market worth of which could feed a family of four for a month in some parts of the world. We have *The Voice* and 3-D printers, and websites that pick out outfits for us and mail them to our front doors. Nobody wants to fight right now.

Fighting is for people who don't give a fuck.

But each time an innocent person dies at the hands of police under questionable circumstances, that equals one less fuck to give.

In middle school, I lost a few fucks because I was alone and seething. And someone told me that I didn't have to sit and take it.

On the corner of Hollywood and Highland, I lost a few fucks because it was ugly and dirty and I was alone, and the music was so disturbing, so well-executed, and so incredibly and viscerally powerful, that it made me into someone I didn't want to be, but truly was.

Since then, they've cleaned that corner up real nice. Put in a Metro Station, got rid of the hookers and the pimps, and opened up some national chains. That corner almost got its fucks back.

But then like an act of nature, like the rain that suddenly sprang up these past few weeks to end the California drought, an "officer involved shooting occurred."

And another one occurred.

And another one occurred.

And another one occurred.

And with each one, we lose a fuck.

With each one, we turn into who we are even if we don't want to be it. And we become ready to punch directly in the mouth whoever or whatever is making us seethe.

In 1987 "Walk This Way" was the breakout single from *Raising Hell*. But it's a lyric from a relatively unknown track that seems most prescient nearly 30 years later.

If you try to take what's mine
I'll take it back y'all.
It's like that.

No wonder I hid that one from the white kids. ✐

CARVELL WALLACE *is a writer and a dad living in the Bay Area.*

SPOT

SOUNDS OF TWO EYES OPENING

Spot's recent book, *Sounds of Two Eyes Opening,* captures the particular vibrancy of Hermosa Beach in the late '70s, where it was the center to the skating, skateboarding, and punk cultures of Southern California. Spot documented the nascence of Black Flag and the incandescence of California girls from native range, which lenses it in a way that refreshes the humanity of two scenes that have long since run aground on cliché representation. The following images are culled from the book, as well as Spot's personal archives.

SPOT SPEAKS

The old Kodak Brownies were fun but I finally figured out they were inadequate to capture the images I saw in my head. By the time I saw the movie *Blow-Up* I had an idea of what I needed—a good SLR. That film was probably the motivation for me to commit to some of my dreams. In 1969 I got a great deal on a brand new Pentax H1a.

Hermosa Beach was a way different world that folks weren't aware of—sure, it was "Surf City," but that's a whole 'nother story. In the grand L.A./Hollywood media eye we didn't exist. There was no flashy disco culture or tourist attractions. In the words of G.S. Oldman, it was "a sad, broken-hearted area of the world where the taverns burned with the dull glare of dying enthusiasm." Maybe that's a little overly poetic but it's an accurate description of what it felt like to live there.

I ended up in Hermosa because I was homeless. Somehow Hermosa offered more couches to crash on, and some guys were building a recording studio. Aside from being cheap transportation, rollerskating was a great way to put the outdoor world to use and to conduct experiments in gravity, velocity, traction, and immovable objects. In other words—fun. Skateboarders, bicyclists, and runners were just part of the overall landscape. Then there were some sketchy stoner rockers playing unspeakable music and doing unspeakable things out of sight inside the old, dilapidated bath house on the Strand. I was entrusted with the secret knock. I wasn't a static spectator; I was part of the entire thing happening around me.

[The people I photographed] were people I skated with, partied with, lived with, drank with, got stupid with, got hurt with, worked up a lotta sweat with, and occasionally did laundry with. We had to do laundry every once in a while. It was rare when any of us actually took off our skates to do it. We skated through grocery stores and ran up and down stairs that way.

Back then, there wasn't much interest in any of these photos. I knew I had to move on and do other things and wait for the time to come to me. I was doing stuff that was important to me whether anyone paid attention to it or not.

—AS TOLD TO JESSICA HOPPER

From Teklife to the Next Life

BY MEAGHAN GARVEY

The basement of DJ Spinn's childhood home—the house where his mom still lives in Markham, Illinois—isn't just his lifelong studio. It's a living museum of footwork, juke, and ghetto house history. Its wood-panelled walls are decked in posters, faded from smoke but still intact, from parties stretching back nearly two decades.

His favorite hangs near the staircase, back when he went by "Spin": it's from 1997, his first time playing Chicago's legendary Bud Billiken parade, the annual late-summer celebration where house music blasts through the streets of the Bronzeville neighborhood. Somewhere upstairs, his mom has stored archives of videos from his grade school musicals and clarinet performances. Along with DJ Rashad, DJ Tre, DJ Manny, and Gant-Man, he's one of the original members of Ghettoteknitianz, the ever-expanding footwork crew that would ultimately rebrand as Teklife in 2010 before they'd proceed to steadily take over the worldwide dance underground. Every available space in Spinn's basement studio is crammed with a vast array of mixers, MPCs, samplers, dusty 4-tracks—gear that was shared among the crew for years until they could afford their own. It's all here, in this inconspicuous basement in the south suburb of Markham. The only thing missing is Rashad.

A couple minutes down the Dixie Highway is Markham Roller Rink, where 10-year-old Spinn, born Morris Harper, learned how to dance and first encountered Rashad Harden, then 11 and already DJing at the rink and on WKKC's precocious Saturday morning ghetto house showcase, *The Young People's Network.*" "Man, everybody used to be at Markham Roller Rink, that was the spot," says Spinn, now 34. "Every Saturday they had the disco, and that's where pretty much all my friends met up." For decades Chicago was a premiere city for urban rollerskating culture: There were rinks all over the southside, and a signature style—"JB," named for the James Brown remixes that often provided the soundtrack—characterized by super-technical footwork routines. Years later, Spinn, Rashad, and Tre

would hunt for home-recorded tapes (when Dance Mania Records shuttered in '99, mixtape deals were all the rave) circulating from rink to rink. Fitness Factory on 87th, Dr. Martin Luther King Jr. Center on 76th, Glenwood Roller Rink near 195th. "We'd go to every roller rink around town, trying to soak up culture. *Oh, they footworking like this over here.* That was the club before the club," Spinn recalls. Some have long since shuttered; Markham, one of the country's first black-owned rinks, got bought out and renovated by the city in 2012. "There's not the interest anymore that there used to be," says Tre. "Times have definitely changed."

Change has been a constant for the Teklife family in the last handful of years, and for Spinn especially. He's rarely in the same place for too long these days. He and Rashad embarked with cautious optimism on their first tour abroad in early 2011, around the time of Planet Mu's first *Bangs & Works* compilation, which served as footwork's international debut. They were Teklife's evangelists, and they were going to make you a believer. "Just like at home, it was back to baby steps—back to when we first started playing and people was like, *What the fuck is this shit?*" Spinn laughs. They had their ways: an arsenal of what they called "grease" tracks, guaranteed party pleasers and familiar four-on-the-floor patterns, sandwiched around the raw shit. But it turned out Europe liked the raw shit, the *tracks*, the stuff these guys were making in each other's basements to bring to Battle Groundz every Sunday. The uninitiated rarely knew how to dance to it—in Earl's basement earlier in the week, DJ Earl and DJ Taye (two of Teklife's youngest members) busted out impressions of first-time footwork attempts reminiscent of that YouTube video of

PREVIOUS & OPPOSITE PAGES: PHOTO BY DAVID SAMPSON

L→R JAMAL OLIVER (LITEBULB), EARL LAPLACE III (DJ TRE), DEMPSEY BARNEY & MORRIS HARPER (DJ SPINN)

the cybergoth underpass dance party—but they could *feel* it. Tre had no idea anyone outside of the country knew his music until Rashad reported back from Paris and Belgium: People were shouting his name.

Soon Spinn and Rashad were touring around the world throughout spring and fall, then part of summer, a little winter. Spinn learned from Rashad's mistakes regarding British immigration: "If you ever need to get into England, just say you're going to a wedding," he says, laughing. "I'm cool now, I got a work visa, but back then I had a whole script". Spinn has stories on stories: he and Rashad, tearing through Europe, Asia, South America, preaching the word of Chicago and having a blast. They were sketching a blueprint for the rest of Teklife to follow, cobbling together a diehard global fanbase. They were making it up as they went along, but they had each other's backs. He cracks up remembering their first trip to Kiev, where some kids in the street had clearly never seen a black person before and where,

after a successful show, Spinn challenged Rashad to a drinking contest. "I wake up and Rashad is splashing me with this little bucket and throws me some pants. *Bro, ya got drunk and pissed your pants on the floor!* I said, *Whaaat!* He said, *Bro, we got pictures. But beyond that—you gotta know I love your pussy ass, 'cause I went and walked in motherfucking 100 degrees to get your ass a pair of pants!* And if you don't know nothing about Kiev, it's hills—fuck San Francisco, like mountain hills! That's when I found out whiskey is my demon liquor, and I ain't never got that drunk again—well, okay, I got that drunk at South by Southwest last year." Tre nods knowingly: "That was like *The Hangover* all over again."

But back home, reality sets in, always. It was never just about Spinn or Rashad. From day one, the good of the crew at large has trumped any individual measures of success: If they were going to get on, they were going to get on together. You don't have to look much further than the tracklist of *Double Cup*, Rashad's

MEAGHAN GARVEY

2013 magnum opus, an album that redefined foot-work to the masses as something limitless, nuanced, unprecedentedly smooth. Listed boldly, not in the fine print but as featured artists, are Earl, Taye, Man-ny, DJ Phil, and Teklife's Bay Area constituent, Taso; Spinn is featured on eight of the 14 tracks. It was Rashad's album, but it was *everybody's* album—it was a Teklife album.

Some of Teklife's members are separated in age by more than 10 years. Earl, who started producing at 12 and joined the crew in 2008, is 24 now; Taye, the young-est, is 20. For them, Teklife's first generation have served as big brothers as much as collaborators. Earl and Taye were welcomed into the crew with open arms, from the time they were wide-eyed admirers who'd come to see their icons turn Battle Groundz out every Sunday, watching Rashad run back tracks over and over again at the behest of the dancers. Rashad's first words to both of them, they recall with a laugh: "How long you been making tracks, bro?" He was the guy who'd made tracks that had changed their perspective on music, and his faith in them gave them confidence in themselves. That sense of mentorship has accompanied the music for as long as Teklife's existed. On "R House," a 2011 collab-oration between Rashad and Manny, a sample from a 1987 house track, Rhythm Controll's "My House," gets flipped to a defiant plural possessive: *This is OUR house!* "It's family first. Period," says Spinn emphatically. "You gotta find somebody like you to be like you, if you want it to carry on."

Rashad's absence carves out a tangible space in Spinn's basement studio, just as it did in Earl's base-ment studio the day before, the *Double Cup* vinyl loom-ing quietly over his computer monitor. Less than two years ago, Rashad was hopping down the stairs on one leg after a serious car accident that forced him to cancel his European fall tour, so he, Earl, and Taye could re-cord "Bombaklot," their contribution to the *Hyperdub 10.1* compilation. You can hear Rashad in little man-nerisms shared naturally among the crew: the specif-ic way he'd say "bro," or the regular invocation of his mantra, "no lacking." "Sometimes at shows, I just hear his voice in my head, like, *Ay dog, you better kill!*" says Earl. His voice is still there in vocal samples on tracks spanning decades; the crew has preserved troves of his unreleased tracks across their hard drives, flash drives, and mixtapes. But on April 26, 2014, Rashad was found unresponsive in an apartment on Chicago's westside,

and he died from what was later ruled a drug overdose. After having been denied entry into Canada the night before, he was supposed to meet Spinn in Detroit; they were playing a show with Taye and ghettotech legend DJ Godfather, who had helped Rashad and Spinn coin the "Ghettoteknitianz" moniker a decade prior. Rashad didn't show up in Detroit that day. The crew would nev-er see him again.

Nobody is exactly sure how to talk about Teklife with-out Rashad, because that was never supposed to happen.

———

Spinn had seen Rashad at Markham Roller Rink for a few years, but their official introduction wasn't until Spinn's first day of his freshman year at Thorn-wood High School. They bonded over the boombox in their homeroom class, the resident music dudes. Spinn showed Rashad—already a pretty established DJ for a kid not yet old enough to drive—some mixes he'd made from meticulously blending specific sections of other people's mixtapes together with a setup he'd concocted from his mom's entertainment system. When Rashad revealed he had turntables at his house, Spinn's world truly came to life. He laughs remembering his first time visiting Rashad's house, his mind blown by the two-channel mixer and drum machine, before finding out Rashad was grounded when his dad came home early and Rashad tried to hide behind the refrigerator.

The pair held dance practice on a daily basis, and Rashad showed Spinn how to use turntables and make beats. Everyone was broke; if you had gear, you shared it with your friends. Tre (who first met Spinn outside a nearby Fuddruckers) brought around his MPC for years until Spinn could afford his own; DJ Malcolm, who'd spin at the Markham Rink, had a bunch of MIDI keyboards; they'd ditch school to come through and mess with them. "We ain't know what we was doing," said Spinn. "We just knew that if we could say *bitch* and *muthafucka* and put it in keys—oh, it was over! We was having fun, we just wanted to be young and do something." They idolized ghetto house heroes DJ Milton and DJ Deeon, guys who were throwing parties in the projects, where Rashad, Spinn, and Tre, three dudes from the suburbs, stuck out like sore thumbs. They joined the prestigious House-O-Matics dance crew, a name shouted out constantly in ghetto house

"We always had these stupid little hurdles: *Oh, you not from the city, you from the 'burbs, I'm from 79th, you from Markham,* you know, the same stuff that go on today. But these were the proving grounds—there wasn't no MySpace, you actually had to go to these places to make your name."

———————————————

PHOTO BY DAVID SAMPSON

DJ SPINN IN HIS HOME STUDIO, 2015

tracks throughout the '90s and beyond, and were introduced to DJ Clent and RP Boo, who—along with Traxman—comprise footwork's holy trinity. Boo played them some tracks he'd been working on that left their heads spinning. Rashad and Spinn started testing out their own tracks, only when they were sure they were cold enough. The dancers were apprising the DJs about what made them go off, which informed the tracks being produced in people's houses—a cycle that sped the evolution of the sound. Rashad and Spinn DJed now-legendary parties at the Elks Lodge on 51st and Prairie—parties thrown by the Gangster Disciples, but all gangs were welcome. As long as no one broke the peace, no one got their ass beat. "We always had these stupid little hurdles: *Oh, you not from the city, you from the 'burbs, I'm from 79th, you from Markham*, you know, the same stuff that go on today. But these were the proving grounds—there wasn't no MySpace, you actually had to go to these places to make your name."

Making a name: The concept is central to so much of Chicago music history, especially music that comes from the city's consistently broken south and west sides. If there's a persistent fallacy about the city, it's that there is a unified Chicago identity its residents can claim en masse. But Chicago is fractured, geographically, socioeconomically, spiritually. In many ways, it's a city disowned from its own realities: It's white kids who've never had a reason to venture farther south on the Red Line than Sox–35th giddily hollering "Chiraq!" And if Chicago doesn't give a fuck about you, it doesn't pretend to. It produces brilliance, but doesn't have the infrastructure to support it. If you want to do something special, you will have to do it yourself with whatever is at your disposal. Even a coveted Kanye co-sign is hardly a guarantee. There's an air of cool resignation here: This is how things are, this is how they will always be. Success here puts a target on your back; when you get some money, you move on to greener coasts. So it goes.

Even today, some parts of the city are functionally invisible to others. It's been that way for the better part of a century, since the Great Migration established Chicago's black and immigrant working class and multiplied the city's black population fivefold. The Chicago Housing Authority grew increasingly restrictive, squeezing the majority of its new black citizens into an overcrowded stretch of slums along State between 18th and 39th known as the Black Belt. Chicago blues emerged as a voice of overworked, underpaid black creatives tired of being relegated less and less space. "I'm gonna tell you what the blues is: When you ain't got no money, you got the blues," Howlin' Wolf said to preface a 1966 performance of "How Many More Years." Decades later, the 1979 Comiskey Park Disco Demolition Night made it clear that the city's loudest and most visible demographic didn't have room for music that wasn't straight, white, rock 'n roll; that same year, the Warehouse—where house music was in its nascence—made room. Ghetto house was a shout from the country's most extreme public housing redevelopment project, constructed by the CHA when it was convenient and then torn down when it wasn't.

Maybe the city wanted to pretend like its less-inviting neighborhoods didn't exist, but tracks like Parris Mitchell's "Ghetto Shout Out!!" wrote these places back into the city's history. "Robert Taylor's in this motherfucker (hell yea!)"—the largest public housing project in the country upon its completion in '62, named for a black housing activist who resigned as the CHA's chairman when it became clear that integration was never the city council's priority. "Cabrini-Green's in this motherfucker (hell yea!)"—situated on a northside strip that's now mostly condos, they were the last projects to be demolished under the CHA's Plan For Transformation (a plan that mostly served to displace families from their homes). Juke wedged its way onto the radio; it may have been in tiny bursts, as on WGCI's *20 Second Workout* segment ("You used to get 20 seconds! *Work it work it work it work it!*" Spinn laughs), but it was something. And still, there's a sense of dissociation that doesn't seem to go away. There are stretches of Chicago full of people who have, in all likelihood, never heard a footwork track in their life, completely cut off from the genius coming out of their own city.

Footwork as a culture rests on that foundation, and in all its complexities, it reflects the sometimes contradictory nature of its hometown. It's technical but resourceful, reality-grounded but avant-garde, community-oriented yet competitive, globally scalable but Chicago to the core. It's a positive legacy left by a city that never did shit for you, but remains a part of you all the same. "I'm Chicago all day because this is my life. It's the place that made me," said Spinn. "That's always been important to us: namesake. To leave your mark. That's just the school we come from, the old school. People nowadays, they'll skirmish their name up just to get a dollar. Nah, man—integrity, and how I feel on the inside about my-

He didn't want to sit in his hotel room in silence, he wanted to play some fuck-ing tracks. "Looking at Taye in his eyes, the young dude, how he was looking—— I know he needed this too," he said.

———————————————

self? I ain't about to compromise that for nothing. Ain't nothing like respect." In the case of Teklife, that legacy isn't just yours, but a mark you couldn't have made alone, that could have been made no other way.

———————

By 2013, Teklife's presence had been solidly established in Chicago and was extending exponentially worldwide. Rashad and Spinn were touring half the year, returning with a redoubled seriousness each time. Earl, Taye, Tre, Manny, and the rest of the quickly expanding crew were starting to get national and international bookings themselves, armed with flash drives full of straight heat lent from Rashad with love. New to the roster, Taso invited Rashad and Spinn to San Francisco to track out for the winter. They began working on the batch of tracks that would ultimately lead to *Double Cup* in a window-filled studio overlooking the Bay, all the way out to Oakland—and the tracks were magical. "We was smoking so much fucking weed, getting all fucked up," Spinn said, laughing. "I felt like I was just floating on a cloud—looking out the window, feeling like we was flying! And it was just like, man, this the direction right here." Their signature triplet patterns (established well before EDM-trap made it trendy, or something, again) were countered with a half-time, West coast–inspired pace. "It was versatility, showing all the different angles of footwork and all the influences they picked up over the years from traveling," said Earl. "And it was a statement that footwork is not what the media was making it out to be, either—hardcore, or unproduced, or over-produced, or whatever. It was dope producers from Chicago pushing this culture, and this was just one way to do it."

Double Cup was a game-changer. It was footwork like the world had never heard it before: an album in the truest sense, in a genre that had often felt too ephemeral for the format. It was footwork you could wash dishes to, footwork you could make out to, footwork that could charm the most conservative of ears. It thrashed and bucked: *I don't give a fuck about you, I don't give a fuck about myself*, a *Juice* sample spat on "I Don't Give a Fuck," hi-hats spraying like gunfire. It swooned: On "Let U No," a breathless Floetry sample (*You make me so, so, so, so, so, so…*) felt lightheaded and swirling like a drunken first kiss. Mostly, it soared. The album cover was no coincidence: a jet's-eye view of Chicago's golden-orange, sodium vapor–lit grid—the broken city blurring together, for the moment, into a glowing, triumphant composite. And though this music was unmistakably Chicago, it invited the world to join, with a generousness the city rarely shows its own people. To hear the flushed, syrupy Rhodes stabs of "Feelin" blasting out of sweaty Brooklyn warehouses was its own triumph: snobby East coast hipsters losing their collective shit to the sounds of a black Midwestern avant-garde that had long gone uncelebrated but kept going anyway. It was a win for a city in serious need of a win, and for a dude who more than deserved it.

2014 was going to be Teklife's year—not just for its primary ambassadors Rashad and Spinn, but for the entire crew. They destroyed SXSW, playing (by Spinn's count) an unfathomable 21 shows. "We were just toasting to success," said Tre. "We had a ball, and I knew everything was going to be huge from that point forward. I would just think of the days when we would be in Spinn's house for hours, up all night just making tracks—all that work is starting to pay off." Earl and Taye were both in the midst of prolific streaks, establishing themselves as promising voices of Teklife's second generation. Spinn and Manny went back out to the West Coast. Rashad was bouncing around, touring Japan in January, coming home for a day or two, heading off to South America. Still, he was in constant contact with the rest of the crew. Tre remembers Rashad Skyping him for hours from Brazil with Machinedrum, talking about how they were finally in the positions for both of their sons to be set. "When he got back, he was super tired, you could just hear it in his voice," said Spinn. "I was like, *Bro, I think you should get some sleep*, and he was like, *Nah man, I'm good, I got shit to do*. We had a little bit of time before we went on tour together, and I ain't think nothing of anything, it was all good."

Rashad couldn't get into Canada, so Spinn went on ahead. They planned to meet in Detroit for the next day's show. Spinn didn't know Rashad was heading back to Chicago first; their last conversation was about customs. The next day Spinn took a train from Toronto to Detroit, anticipating that he'd meet Rashad there; his phone didn't work in Canada. Boylan, another Teklife member and a science teacher at Rashad and Spinn's old high school, finally got through. Spinn knew it was going to be about Rashad. "He got on FaceTime and told me what he thought was going on, and I'm on the train

PHOTO BY EREZ AVISSAR

DJ SPINN AND RASHAD IN AUSTIN, TEXAS, 2014

Rashad's absence carves out a tangible space in Spinn's basement studio, just as it did in Earl's basement studio the day before, the Double Cup vinyl looming quietly over his computer monitor.

_____

trying not to freak out and cuss him out. *What are you telling me, bro? Where is Rashad right now? You telling me what you think is going on, but until I know somebody seen him and can tell me this is what this is...*

Earl was at home, having woken up with a strange feeling. Then he got the call. "I couldn't even think straight," he said. "I called Spinn and he was in transit to go meet Taye. And then Taye called me like, *Bro, please don't tell me this is real.* And that was one of the most painful moments of my life."

In Detroit, the promoters were planning to cancel the show, but Spinn declined. He didn't want to sit in his hotel room in silence, he wanted to play some fucking tracks. "Looking at Taye in his eyes, the young dude, how he was looking—I know he needed this too," he said. "I couldn't fucking digest it at the time. Because I didn't get to see him. And I never got to see him again." Rashad's family opted not to have a funeral.

The night went... it's hard to say. Taye's voice shrinks to barely a whisper revisiting it. They got through the show. If the crowd hadn't known what had happened when they got there, they knew when they left. DJ Godfather picked them up afterward and they talked for a while. "It was a lot of love in Detroit," Spinn remembers. "Everybody was feeling this shit. And through the somberness of it all, I was smiling on the inside a little bit." But everything had changed.

———

For a while, nobody made tracks. It wasn't even an option. "Everything I ever learned from Rashad hit me at the same time," said Earl. "You hit the studio and gather your thoughts, and I sat down and I was so overtaken, I couldn't even remember how to make tracks. I'm serious. I sat down and was like, *How do I do this without Rashad?*" Spinn couldn't think about it either: "Fuck that shit, I didn't know what to make a track about after that. You know, we get fucked up and we have a good time and we give you an instruction book to have a fuckin' great time."

Rashad's autopsy results were inconclusive for months. Ultimately the cause of death was ruled an accidental overdose, with the toxicology reports citing heroin, cocaine, and alprazolam (Xanax) intoxication. Spinn maintains that it wasn't until shortly before Rashad's death that anyone had much of an idea that he was using hard drugs. "Things started add-

ing up," says Spinn. "Behavior. Being real sleepy. Never coming round, or when he did being a little different. A little weird." For months Spinn wrote it off because of all the touring and late nights and gigs; Spinn was fatigued and near exhaustion himself. But now he realizes that he was just too close to see it. "I was with him every single day."

News of Rashad's death rocked Chicago and far beyond, in every city that had ever been blessed with a DJ set from the Teklife ambassador. Anyone tangentially involved in dance music had a Rashad story. The night after his death, I heard "I'm Gone," a highlight off Rashad's 2011 album *Just a Taste*, ring out across an unusually somber Bushwick club, with its heartbroken Gil Scott-Heron sample: "I left three days ago, but no one seems to know I'm goooone..." Tributes sprang up across the world: a Boiler Room homage in London with sets from his close friends and collaborators at Hyperdub, heartfelt written remembrances from DJs and music lovers worldwide, endless memorial mixes. But Rashad's death was felt nowhere sharper than in Chicago: His loss was the city's loss. April had been ushered in cruelly with the death of Frankie Knuckles, the godfather of house, a true pioneer who'd remained active in Chicago's dance music scene for more than 30 years. Losing Frankie meant losing one of the most essential parts of Chicago's cultural history. But losing Rashad, somehow, cut deeper. Even with all he'd achieved, it was painfully obvious we'd only gotten a glimpse of his brilliance.

———

Months later, out in California with Taso, Spinn heard a song playing on CVS' speakers and immediately knew it was Rashad talking to him. It was a sample he'd never placed before, from an old Rashad track called "Burn That Bitch." He went back to the studio and flipped the same sample as a tribute. The track would eventually become Spinn's contribution to *Next Life*, the Teklife compilation-cum-memorial released in late 2014 on Hyperdub, the proceeds of which go to Rashad's son Chad. Spinn and Earl had a talk—"a very real talk," Earl recalled. "And he said, you know what Rashad was about, and you know what Rashad would say if he was here: *Man, what y'all sad for? Keep making the music, no lacking, just keep going and make sure Teklife is where it needs to be.* It's the message the he's instilled in all of us, and because he's not here, we want to be that spirit." For the first time in Spinn's adult life, he was making music without Rashad as his other half.

Less than three months later, almost like a condolence from the universe, Spinn became a dad. His girl asked him to choose a name. "And I remember having this conversation with Rashad before he passed, before we went on tour. He was asking me, because we had gotten into a little disagreement about some shit. Mostly I had to question him about some drug shit. We had a real talk, and he opened up to me about some shit that I didn't know about. And he asked me: *After this shit, man, am I still the godfather of your son?* And I'm like, *What? Bro, shut the fuck up, that's a dumb-ass question.* After he passed, that moment right there kept playing back in my head. *Am I still the godfather?* And that's the moment I knew."

Rashad Harper was born on July 14, 2014. Chad, who just turned 10, adores him. "Man, he couldn't wait to meet my son. That shit was adorable," Spinn smiles. "They got to be friends one day, that's just inevitable. They got an age difference, but shit, that's the little homie." Spinn still needs to drop off Chad's birthday gift, since he's been out of town for so long. "All he wanna do is make music, so I gotta go get him this drum machine from Gant. He's got Rashad's old drum machine." Chad is now the same age Rashad was when he started to DJ.

Life has gone on because it's had to. Earl and Taye traveled to Seoul this winter, following the trail Rashad and Spinn blazed—they can't get enough of footwork in Asia, dancing and all. They're both in grind mode, prepping for their respective debut albums, both currently untitled. Tre's putting the finishing touches on his next EP, *The Underdog*, along with a split EP with Earl. A Teklife-produced rap album—*Live From Yo Momma's House*, in collaboration with Treated Crew's Mic Terror—is in the works for later this year. They're working out how to more thoroughly incorporate footwork dancing into their live shows, something Rashad had been advocating for a while. Their work ethic has been keen for years, but their mindset is sharper now that both Teklife's legacy and Rashad's rest with them. They all still feel his presence: "When I make music, I do it as if he was sitting here listening," says Taye. "I do it with everything he taught me. Just like he was still here. He lives with us." Rashad's influence on Teklife's second generation isn't just musical; his example helped shape Earl and Taye into the driven, positive,

and deeply loyal adults they have become. "My life would not be the same without him," says Earl. "Rashad always put everybody before him. He was for everybody. As long as you were positive and living to your fullest potential, he was willing to help you out. We want to be that spirit that carries on his message."

Spinn doesn't really like talking about DJ Spinn, singular. "*Oh, I'm DJ Spinn, and this the DJ Spinn show*—nah, I don't really even like to say my name that much, it's weird," he admits. "You know who I am. It's a Teklife show." But he is now Teklife's most prominent ambassador, a spotlight he is learning to stand in without his lifelong foil beside him. His first official solo release since Rashad passed, an EP called *Off That Loud*, will be released on Hyperdub this spring; his debut full-length on Hyperdub is due out later this year. The snippets he previews, filling every wood-paneled corner of his mom's basement, are transcendent. There's live instrumentation from Spinn's cousin, drifting organically before coalescing into an impossibly detailed beat. Another track features breathtaking vocals from Canadian singer Kiesza that sounds like a visitation from Aaliyah's ghost; it's 160 BPM but barely registers as footwork at all until, suddenly, it hits you. It doesn't feel right to compare it to *Double Cup*—would anything?—but this much is clear: It's the next chapter in Teklife's history.

Spinn bears the weight of Rashad's absence with almost startling grace. He is generous with his memories of his best friend and almost always punctuates them with laughter and deep-drawling Rashad impressions. In these memories the two often blur together into one person, picking up where the other left off; when Rashad would fall asleep at the MPC—as he did regularly—Spinn would keep working ahead. People don't really do groups anymore, Spinn notes, especially not in Chicago. "People break up and carry on, fight over stupid shit," he notes. "Rashad, that was the most loyal person I knew. He was real. You might not like everything he did—we argued, that was me and him! I needed that rough-edged cat around me. He was never out here to betray nobody. He was always a real friend, even to people that weren't real friends to him. He was loyal, and generous like a motherfucker. He was a part of my whole life." ✏

MEAGHAN GARVEY *is a Contributing Editor at* Pitchfork. *Her mom grew up a few blocks away from DJ Spinn's studio.*

The Passion of Antony Hegarty

BY HAZEL CILLS

PHOTO BY JACK PIERSON

You are my sister, and I love you," Antony Hegarty sang on her breakthrough 2005 album *I Am a Bird Now*; "May all of your dreams come true, I want this for you." It's a deceptively simple lyric on the page, but there's a soulful insistence to Hegarty's voice that conveys belief in the face of pain and fear. "You Are My Sister" is the musical equivalent of a woman's outstretched hand, waiting to be held by a fellow woman looking for solidarity, for acceptance. This metaphorical gesture has defined much of Hegarty's work over the past two decades.

The England-born, California-raised artist moved to New York City back in the early '90s to pursue academic studies in experimental theatre. It was there that Hegarty's group Antony and the Johnsons was formed, in 1997. With a multi-octave voice that seemingly embodies an entire church choir, Hegarty has crafted an orchestral musical identity that is as grounded in activism as it is in artistic experimentation; it's easier to describe Hegarty's art career not by its mediums (of which there are many) but by its themes: femininity, spirituality, and the natural world.

In 2005, Antony and the Johnsons won the prestigious Mercury Prize for *I Am A Bird Now*, a dark meditation on gender fluidity, the AIDS crisis, and the safety of gay and trans people at large. The group's next record, *The Crying Light*, was a heartbreaking rumination on the Earth's slow demise. On both albums, Hegarty is unafraid to tackle contemporary issues many songwriters would shy away from or ignore entirely: "I sometimes feel my job has been to hold space for things that people are not ready to talk about," Hegarty told me. "If it was impossible for the culture to address these things, I would keep them alive."

Last year saw the first exhibition put on by Hegarty's art collective, Future Feminism, which featured works from like-minded creators including Kiki Smith and Marina Abramovic, as well as the release of *Turning*, the live film and album documentation of Hegarty's 2006 multimedia performance of the same name. Playing music from her first three albums, Hegarty staged *Turning* as an artistic collaboration with a dozen other women whose genders fell at various points across the spectrum, creating a living, breathing, advancing definition of sisterhood. As the often-brutal experiences of transwomen are just reaching the gates of mainstream media in 2015 through personalities like actress Laverne Cox and television shows like *Transparent*, *Turning* stands as a groundbreaking work of art and a precedent for contemporary culture's exploration of trans-feminism.

Hegarty's stark-white SoHo studio is lined with half-finished paintings, with the tenets of Future Feminism scrawled on the wall. THE FUTURE IS FEMALE, one reads, like both a prediction to the world and a subtle call to arms. During our talk, Hegarty and I both comb our fingers through a shaggy blanket draped across the couch, trying to find a little comfort while discussing violence, politics, and the Earth's forthcoming ecological end—themes that also appear throughout her new record, *Hopelessness*.

Do you feel like you're one of those people who will never leave New York?

I always thought I was one of those people, but I don't know anymore. I've had it.

Did you read the article David Byrne wrote for *The Guardian* about New York's one percent squelching the artistic integrity of the city?

I don't know if you can really blame the one percent. The global economy has changed everything so intensely in the last 15 years, and it's changing where the artists go. With the Internet, you have access to all the same information from Papua, New Guinea, that you have from Second Avenue—everyone can watch the same videos of [performance artist] Leigh Bowery. You don't need the city anymore.

I was part of the last generation that moved to New York out of necessity in order to survive and meet people and share. I came here before the Internet. I moved to the city in desperation. It was the last place in America that I could go, because I knew like-minded people lived here. I knew subversive minds would be festering and actualizing. I came from California, where people were very passive, creatively. I certainly wouldn't recommend that a young person move to New York City now, but then again there are some kids out in Bushwick having a good time. But I don't really know what the quality of their life is, so maybe it's just the generation gap. I've heard about resurgent scenes, but I don't know what the new scene is. In a weird way, I feel like reality is subcultural now—so few people really want to deal with it. Reality is the most subversive thing you can talk about.

What do you mean by that?

Whereas subcultures have been all about fantasy and looking at the way everyone is dressing up and being Other, the one thing that no one is talking about is reality, or at least anything much beyond the reality of their own pedestrian lives. The reality of the big picture right now is that, as a species, we're facilitating this massive extinction event the likes of which haven't been seen for millions of years: 50 percent of the world's species will be extinct by the end of the century. And people just want to try to have a good time and get out of here as quick as they can.

I went over to Björk's house the other day and put the Oculus Rift on my head. It was really disturbing. Virtual reality is something that people are going to be living in in 10 years time. We are going to lose people to that. As the world becomes less palatable, imaginary worlds are going to become more palatable. That's what technology is pushing us toward. Who's going to regulate that? When are we going to step up as a species and identify what our values are? What do we want to become? What are we the victims of becoming? Capitalism is deciding what we're becoming.

Outside of the Future Feminists collective, who are some artists that you feel are engaging with those issues on the same level you are?

A few artists are doing it in more subliminal or careful ways. I think I'm the most full-throttle, honestly, but I'm marginal, so not many people know what I'm doing. I sometimes feel like my job has been to hold space for things that people are not ready to talk about, and then once they start talking about them, I can move on to the next thing. I'm almost ready to move on from the environment, because people are really beginning to realize they're going to die.

Do you feel like artists could do more to bring visibility to the ecological platform than just singing?

Artists should have some courage for a change—stop worrying about getting your money and talk about the deep things you care about. A lot of artist are very, very chicken, especially in America. They don't want to rock the boat. It's no fun being criticized or being seen as a heretic or a harpy. Some people pretend to take big risks in their work but they're not taking any risk at all; they pretend they're revealing these intimate secrets about their lives, and all they're doing is feeding some romantic fog machine, you know? *Talk about reality*. That's my whole thing now. I don't even care about my personal life anymore in terms of self-expression. All I care about is trying to express reality, which is a really different modus operandi for a pop musician.

—

What's your ideal relationship with an audience while you're performing?

That's an excruciating question.

Excruciating in that it changes all the time or that it's impossible to answer?

Honestly, I'm very uncomfortable with the relationship. What I want to happen and what I think happens are probably two different things. What I think happens is that people feel less alone because they hear emotion being voiced. And yet I have a lot of ambivalence about the way that I affect people as a singer—I don't want to manipulate people emotionally but, as an expressive and emotional performer, I feel like I have a certain skill set which can draw people into a beautiful experience.

Do you think it's even possible for an artist not to manipulate their audience?

It's almost impossible because it's feeling and sound. But I want people to come to their own conclusions.The way they process the material is not my affair. All I can do is bring myself to the place where we meet—I can't take responsibility for them. I need them to take responsibility for themselves. I'm just a one person in a circumstance, creating an illusion, a dream space. Something spectral. I want to give people release and relief, yet also let them settle into their more profound selves. That's what's exciting to me about silence and a room full of people: the

> "The thing I notice about nature and other animals is that they're not crying about leaving. They're not going to sit around moaning and crying and complaining that they're disappearing."
>
> —ANTONY

potential for a different kind of space that we can share together. And I'm probably the one who benefits the most from that when it's happening. I have the best seat in the house. It's hard, though, and really hideously embarrassing too.

How is it embarrassing?

It's not natural to be up in front of 2,000 people singing.

Do you feel like how you approach performing has changed?

Yeah, 100 times since I started.

Has it gotten less embarrassing?

No.

You've collaborated with Björk several times, most recently on the duet "Atom Dance" from her album *Vulnicura*. How did that song come about?

We're good friends and she asked me to come out and join her in her studio on one of the Virgin Islands and we just sang together. I improvised my part and put that together for her. She has an unusual idea about the place of a guest voice on her records. It's a little mysterious to me.

How does she use guest voices as opposed to how you use guest voices?

Her style of collaborating is so gentle and yet so specific, and she has an amazing way of collaborating with people with very strong personalities and yet making the work utterly her own. Whereas I tend to feature people in a way that's more about them in a certain way, she really has an amazing way of drawing herself out of everyone.

Who would you want to collaborate with that you haven't yet?

I don't really have a bucket list of people; I don't think I'm that good of a collaborator.

I love a lot of musicians, but I would rather be in the audience, honestly. I do love singing in choirs, so I would love to be a part of a group of voices. That would be the best kind of collaboration I could do. I did a beautiful collaboration with this group of aboriginal women from the West Australian Desert where I went out and sang for them while they painted, and that meant a lot to me. It was just a small group of older women and myself in this shed in the middle of the desert, and it was the greatest collaboration I've done in years. Just meeting people that I would never normally meet. I would love to spend more time exploring relationships with people who don't know my work or really care about Western music. Those women didn't give a shit about my stupid singing voice. They were just like, "Oh, that sounds like how it sounds here after the rain falls." I was like, "Yes!"

You sound much more interested in groups of people coming together and experiencing music rather than people simply listening to you.

I've done both to the extreme. The symphony concert I did was just me on stage, and yet 60 people were hidden behind the curtain. But then the light and images were pouring through me. There's always been a conflict of loathing my own body that makes me want to almost be disembodied—to not be there and yet to be there, to separate the voice form the body. But community has always been really important to me. I've taken great refuge in creative communities with other artists and friends. Working together is my happiest time.

———

A large part of feminism for you is looking at the natural world—Mother Earth—and recognizing that women aren't inclined to destroy it in the same way men do today. It puts into perspective how many systems have been constructed to get in the way of the natural order. Do you think the world is set up to not want the feminine?

Or anything circular. The world is set up hierarchically, with a male sort of military model, so it's very hard to get anything done. It's hard to reorganize ourselves. In so many parts of our world, women are just kept as slaves. This isn't 2,000-year-old news; this is today. There are plenty of women in America who are still nothing more

than sex slaves, being held hostage in hotels next to airports. You could go to New Jersey and probably look up a place where you could go and use slaves online right now. It's pretty dark.

It really is. I remember when I heard about Boko Haram and the kidnapped girls in Nigeria—

It's happening here, too. I wouldn't believe it was possible for a long time, but I've recently been exposed to media that has convinced me that that is a dark, sadistic side of men's nature. Women simply don't manifest in the ways that men do. Women don't hold men hostage as sex slaves. It's just a different species. (chuckles) I mean, there's certainly really gnarly, tough lesbians who would be like, "We can do that too." And I'm like, "Yes, you can. But does the massive majority of women want this?" We just don't roll that way.

The thing about that claim, though, is how women can do everything men can do—but then there's this list of incredibly violent things that we would never do.

I'll never forget when Lil' Kim came out with her first record. She was stepping up so hardcore, to such a misogynist industry, and she was like, "You want to try taking me down? I will take you down just as hard." Or when Nicki Minaj came out with that song and she was like, "I'll rape you." It's like she's trying to create a perimeter of safety for herself in a man's world by using a man's language. To me, her song "Lookin' Ass Nigga" was like the latest in this amazing study of gender in pop music in America and how women are having to "man up" so hardcore and still use their sexuality, but as a weapon—it's like the bulletproof-tits kind of thing. In some ways, seeing women dominating men is like a male-constructed fantasy to alleviate male guilt. There's also a whole subculture of very powerful businessmen whose fantasy is nothing more than to be dominated. But the truth is, they're the ones paying the dominatrix at the end of the day. It's still a form of slavery.

One of the tenants in Future Feminism that we are most proud of involves relieving men of their roles as protectors and predators, because we realized we couldn't ask them to stop preying upon us unless we also stopped asking them to protect us. We have this really deep, almost prehistoric notion that the men are supposed to protect us from wild wolves and predators roaming from the other camps. And as long as we're asking men to protect us, we're attached to the idea that protection and privation are two sides of the same broken system—as long as you need to be protected from men and you need a man to protect you, you're rendered powerless.

And these men, they're all born from women's bodies. They don't come out of thin air. Every one of them popped out of a woman's body. And that is part of the crux of the crisis for a lot of men in a really deep, subconscious way, the horror of that dependency. That was why they sought to appropriate Creation itself, with God creating the world in seven days. They sought to upstream all the feminine creative mysterious processes and recast it as their invention.

―――

What makes up your strength at this point?

My closest friends, who have been my friends for like 20 years. Those are my peeps. I'm lucky I have them. And I seek a lot of guidance from a lot of older women artists I've met in the last 10 years, people who are one or two or three generations older than me. I always had a really strong relationship with my grandmother, too.

Do you have any specific mentors?

No. All my mentors are dead. I take that back. Marina [Abramovic] has been a really good mentor for me. She's been a very caring friend and she's given me good advice.

In terms of performance?

Just in terms of how to take care of myself. You know, there are several different ways of being an artist in this world. There's the privileged, protected male way, or else you're a feminine artist who is just constantly attacked in the most heinous and degrading ways as a result of putting yourself out there. And those great female artists are the ones I relate to. They don't get boys'-club privilege, they don't get that constant pat on the back from everyone. They get raked over the coals on the blogs and in the media. They're always eyed with more suspicion and

with sexism and hatred of femininity, especially asserted femininity. Femininity is fine for a man as long as it can be sexualized and subjugated, but as soon as it starts to assert itself, it becomes a real threat. Even if you look at our American indie white music scene, who were the girls that could break through? Eighty percent of them are the ones men can somehow manipulate and the media can somehow sexualize.

It was a miracle when I got access to daylight culture. It was not supposed to happen. If New York media had its way, I would've never happened. It was a miracle facilitated by Lou Reed and a few other artists, along with a confusion about who or what I was, that just let my music push through for a second and created my career. If people would've known what they were getting into, they might have been too reticent about my identity to really let it happen. I'm very, very lucky that I've had the opportunities I've had. I don't know of anyone else from my world who has had those opportunities.

It's hard to talk about progress when there's still so much to be done, but, because of people like *Orange Is the New Black* actress Laverne Cox, there's more trans visibility in commercial media now than ever. Do you ever think, like, "Look at how far we've come?"

I was very excited about Laverne Cox. After I got the Mercury prize in the mid-2000s, I remember saying, "What you're looking at when you look at me is the frontier of what's possible to be embraced by popular culture, and maybe in a few years it's going to be a trans person of color or Native American transperson." What Laverne Cox is bringing is this incredibly articulate conversation about the nuts and bolts of gender and trans-consciousness and how to process it for straight people. She's also brought this beautiful articulation of the crisis of people of color, which is really unexpected, because of her gift as an orator and just her grace and the way she conducts herself with Katie Couric or whatever. It was just so exciting when she thanked Katie Couric for being teachable. I just thought that was an amazing moment on national television.

Having said that, my issue is that I don't really feel like my body of work, ultimately, is about identity politics, although identity politics play a part in it. I'm also really

"I literally am a kind of feral pagan person. I have an animist relationship with the world and with nature."

—ANTONY

weary of America's obsession with identity politics and the way they're manipulated as a smokescreen for political parties to have their way with us.

You've mentioned contextualizing your music in conversation, but the music itself isn't about identity politics.

My work and the work of Future Feminism was to start to connect the dots. I had a gay classics teacher named Vito Russo who wrote a book called *The Celluloid Closet: The History of Gays and Lesbians in Cinema*, and he said, "You can't fight for gay rights without being a feminist. You can't separate those issues." A lot of gay people don't realize that. And then I got to a point where I thought, "You can't really separate feminism from the concerns of ecology and spirituality." So, for better or for worse, I'm inhaling the big picture in my work. I'm wrestling with the biggest scope that I can manage.

In Future Feminism, you identified yourself as a "witch" and connected it to this idea of being unaccepted by patriarchal religions and being put to death. How did you arrive at that label, and do you still adopt it?

Well, I literally am a kind of feral pagan person. I have an animist relationship with the world and with nature, and it's very real for me. I am not just using the word ironically, although there isn't really a proper word for it. You realize that language is still so inadequate. We end up appropriating words that were once used to hate us to describe ourselves again and again. But where's the dignified word for something that's beautiful and pagan and feminist-centered and connected to the Earth's spirituality that that doesn't evoke snickers and centuries of being executed and the Christian Crusades and every revolting thing that ever happened to us? We started looking to indigenous models, which has its own troublesome appropriations, but for a long time the word for "two spirits" was used to describe person of trans identity. There are beautiful indigenous models and language to talk about things that we don't really have dignified language to talk about.

You say "witch" and you're already in a relationship with Christianity, and I'm not in a relationship with Christianity. I could give a fuck about Christianity. Christianity is not the opposite of my religion—Christianity is just more bullshit. It's not my thing. I exist completely separate from it. I'm really just Earth-based and not a Christian, which is ironic because people always say, "Oh, wow, your voice is so otherworldly." And It's like, "Actually, I come from right here." This is it. You guys might be fucking off to paradise elsewhere, but I'm probably not. I'm from right here. This is what I'm made out of, and that's why I'm so concerned—because I'm more invested in this place than a lot of people. People think they're just here for seven years and then they're going to piss off to the unknown, but I have no reason to believe that I'll be anywhere but here in some other manifestation. ✎

HAZEL CILLS *is a staff writer for* Rookie.

Happy Woman Blues

For four decades, Lucinda Williams played and lost games with major labels and major romance. Now, at 62, she has self-released a masterpiece.

BY GRAYSON HAVER CURRIN

When Lucinda Williams was introduced at the Carolina Theatre in Durham, North Carolina, on the night of her 62nd birthday, a brief and awkward pause followed her name.

The seated crowd first looked on stage, of course, but she didn't appear. Audience members shifted their bodies in their padded wooden seats and turned toward the exits, scanning the aisles for a glimpse of one of the sharpest songwriters ever to come from the American South, in hopes she might saunter past them. The throng stared for a second at a woman about Williams' height and age who happened to be returning from the lobby. She ducked quickly into a row, as if embarrassed by not being the star of the show.

Onstage, Robert Milazzo, the director of the Modern School of Film, paused, laughed, and called out for Tom Overby—Williams' husband of five years and manager for just a bit longer. Overby signaled from an alcove that it would be a few moments; the attendees laughed, a trace of anxiety evident in the ripple. Williams was in town not for a concert but instead for a screening of and conversation about *Wise Blood*, a quizzical and dated adaptation of Flannery O'Connor's first novel.

The room was ready to hear from the singer, whether or not she sang any songs.

"She is here," Milazzo offered after a few more minutes, his smile growing more angular. "I promise."

Williams finally walked out onto the stage wearing dark grey jeans and a black jacket, clutching a celebratory glass of wine and taking her time to ease into her chair. The tension vanished. She talked about *Wise Blood*, sure, but mostly she discussed her life and worldview—about her poet father Miller Williams, who took a young Lucinda to meet O'Connor and see her peacocks; about Bob Dylan and Van Morrison, former tourmates who taught her how *not* to lead a band through their own bad examples; about her three Grammys, and how she was disappointed when her 2014 offering, *Down Where the Spirit Meets the Bone*, didn't earn a nomination.

She took questions from the crowd, eased her way through a few acoustic numbers, and indulged the pandering Milazzo. When he asked about religion, her answer alone made the wait worthwhile.

"None of my songs mention Jesus. It's all God. It's non-denominational, so anyone can join," she said.

Williams speaks a little like she sings, leaving considerate pauses between short sentences delivered in the low, scratched twang that helped make her famous.

She's thinking, but it feels as if she's allowing you time to process what she has just said.

"The Bible," she concluded wryly, "is great fodder for songs."

Williams has been making good on running late for most of her life. In fact, in 2014 at the age of 61, she countered any assumption of obsolescence with *Down Where the Spirit Meets the Bone*, one of the most audacious efforts of her career. The double album possesses both a youthful verve and a mature nerve, as Williams doles out wisdom in her rutted, red-clay drawl over the rippling arrangements of a great rock band. When she cut those records, she made enough music for a third disc, due out later this year. Maybe it's too much to say that Williams is in the prime of her career, but at 62 she commands powers of observation and delivery that most singers and songwriters will never reach.

Again, she has taken her time getting here: Booted from high school, she would subsequently drop out of a cultural anthropology program at the University of Arkansas and spend her teenage years in the '70s pinballing between Austin, Houston, and New Orleans. She wrote some songs and performed them alongside deep Delta blues covers—first on street corners and, eventually, in Houston's folk clubs or most anywhere that would have her.

Williams released her first album, a collection of fierce acoustic standards and obscurities called *Ramblin'*, in 1979 at the age of 26. But the next two decades were rife with fits and starts, as she bounced between record labels and failed deals. Despite a critically lauded self-titled disc in the late '80s and a 1994 Grammy for writing Mary Chapin Carpenter's country-radio hit "Passionate Kisses," Williams didn't gain widespread acclaim or much in the way of financial reward until 1998. That's when *Car Wheels on a Gravel Road* pushed her into *Time* magazine, near the top of most every critic's year-end list, and, with her short shock of black hair and leather vest suggesting a honky-tonk Joan Jett, onto *Saturday Night Live*.

She was 45, singing a song about being dumped and becoming apoplectic in the process. "Feels like I been shot," she hollered during the biggest, shortest set of her life, "and I didn't fall down." Those tortured feelings served as the necessary bait for Williams' eventual ascent. A year before the *Saturday Night Live* stop, the *New York Times* titled its piece about the laborious, fraught, and much-delayed process of making *Car Wheels on a Gravel Road*, "Lucinda Williams Is in Pain." And in his tangential 11,000-word *New Yorker* ode to Williams, her South, and her existential complications, Bill Buford wrote, "[Her songs] are unforgiving because they are so relentlessly about pain or longing or can't-get-it-out-of-your-head sexual desire, but most often they're about loss, and usually about losing some impossible fuckup of a man."

Buford detailed the boyfriends who had died or been dismissed, and another who hung precariously in the balance only to, by article's end, join the swollen ranks of Williams' exes. Those bust-ups fueled many of the songs that became standards, like "Side of the Road," the self-reliance proclamation where Williams just needs to feel alive by being alone for a while.

A day after the Carolina Theatre screening, sitting in the bar of Durham's most genteel hotel, Williams revisits the topic. "When I was younger, I would just get lost in these relationships, and my writing would be the first thing to go out the window," she says. "I would feel stuck. I would feel uninspired. That would be my test: If I can't write *in* a relationship, it's the wrong relationship."

Songs would follow in the wake of the breakup. Or, as Buford concluded, "That happiness thing, who needs it?" Turns out, just maybe, Lucinda Williams at least *wants* it: During the last decade, she has entered a new phase of her life and career, the sort of settling-down and settling-in mode that most tend to have before they've passed the half-century mark or before they've buried a dozen friends.

In the past, Williams says, she's never had a steady relationship that not only allowed her to write but even encouraged her to do so; Overby is her first and, perhaps not coincidentally, the longest commitment of her life. She now has more songs in the works than at any other time in her career, even though she wrote her first number (a precious ballad about autumn called "The Wind Blows") when she was 13. Overby helps her screen new demos and has even begun digging through boxes of abandoned archives, rediscovering songs she long ago forsook.

She speaks about the dynamic with a mix of adoration and admiration, regarding Overby as much as a life partner as a lover. In Williams' songs, relationships are lascivious and vicious things; when she talks about Overby, you get the sense that the concept of nurturing remains a new one for her. These days, she's writing real-life love songs.

"When people found out Tom and I were engaged, everybody asked, 'Are you still going to be able to write songs?' It just drove me crazy," she says, pounding an open hand on the dark wooden table. "People are so stuck in the idea that you have to suffer to create, and that's true, but we all suffer. Just because I'm married doesn't mean I'm always going to be happy. From the moment of birth, the doctor slaps you, and you cry. That's what life is."

A week later, at her home in Los Angeles, she tries to explain why it's taken her so long to get places—to a record deal, to success, to stability, to a marriage that integrates all of it. Every few words her voice peaks, as if searching the horizon for an easy answer, the same solution for which she's been looking for four decades.

"People say, 'You're 62, and you're still writing like this?' I'm an anomaly. I should just be retired at this point," she says. "But I'm still growing. I don't know why that is. Some people get old and some people don't. I can't even believe I'm sitting here talking about being old."

Three weeks before Lucinda Williams finally stepped on the stage of the Carolina Theatre last January, she received some news she'd been expecting: On New Year's Day, her father, Miller, had died in Fayetteville, Arkansas, just months after being moved to a nursing home for people with dementia. He was 84.

Williams' parents divorced when she was a child, though they continued living together for several years. When she left high school, Miller homeschooled her by prescribing a list of mandatory reading. When she got into music, he nurtured the interest. When she talks about him now, she talks about his mind—how sharp and bright it was, how analytical he tended to be, how defiant he remained. She makes him sound like a saint.

Yet when he died, she admits, she cried less than she thought she would have. Williams had shed most of her tears months before, during one of her final visits with her father in Fayetteville. She sat on the sun porch that day, her father's arm around her neck and a glass of wine in her hand as the sun began to set in the late afternoon. He told her that he was getting weaker and that, in his advanced age, he could no longer write poetry.

"I cried like a baby," Williams says of that day. "That was the hardest thing. That part of him was gone."

PHOTO BY EMILY BERL

During a subsequent visit late last year, she played a show in Fayetteville, but he was too frail to attend. She played a private set for him and some old friends at home. She sang "Compassion," the acoustic number based on his poem of the same name that opens *Down Where the Spirit Meets the Bone*. In turn, he read the poem. "You don't know what kind of wars are going on / Down where the spirit meets the bone," she sang and he recited. Overby recorded it so that she would never forget.

His poetry—"that part," as she puts it—is perhaps the biggest unifying influence on Williams' output as a Southern songwriter and her attitude as a defiant survivalist, if not in terms of language or aesthetics. Their views on writing, Williams concedes, could be diametric; Miller hated the Beats, for instance, though she liked their romance and adventurousness. His methodical approach to scenes and sentiments applies little to the emotional battlegrounds of her songs. But for both Miller and Lucinda Williams, writing became a rite of life, a necessity akin to breathing, no matter how futile the results could seem.

"My dad said once that poets didn't start getting respected until they were in their 50s or 60s," she says. "With my dad and his writer friends in that world, age wasn't part of the equation."

Miller Williams eventually earned tenure as a professor at his alma mater, the University of Arkansas. In 1990 he won the Poet's Prize, one of America's premier awards for writers, and he read "Of History and Hope" at Bill Clinton's second presidential inauguration seven years later. However, the path to that prestige was circuitous and trying.

As a teenager, he'd been told he had a mathematical mind and that he should pursue science instead of the arts. He studied biology and eventually taught biochemistry; Lucinda remembers how he'd bring home lab rats and anatomical models to show the kids. Miller's politically defiant viewpoints clashed with the entrenched conservatism of the 1950s and '60s Deep South, and he bounced from school to school, his family living like that of a circuit preacher. At one, his review of an Anne Sexton poem about masturbation—"I am spread out. I crucify / My little plum is what you said / At night, alone, I marry the bed."—put him at odds with administrators. He soon quit.

"When you're just starting out as a professor, you teach for a year or two here or a year or two there—at least that's the way it was always explained to me," she says. "But when he achieved tenure at the University of Arkansas, he was there from that moment on."

When Lucinda tries to recount everywhere she lived as a child, she starts and stops, rewinds and resumes, counts backward from the years her two siblings were born and forward from when she began school.

Lake Charles, Louisiana; Vicksburg, Mississippi; Jackson, Mississippi; Atlanta, Georgia; Macon, Georgia; Iowa, Louisiana; Santiago, Chile; Baton Rouge, Louisiana; New Orleans, Louisiana; Mexico City, Mexico; and, at last, Fayetteville, Arkansas. Lying down in the bunk of her tour bus, several weeks into a run up and down the West Coast, it takes about seven minutes.

Miller's movements offered his daughter a veritable tour of the American South. She met the pantheon of the best Southern writers and fell in love with the region's idiosyncrasies and obstinacy. Although the experience sometimes felt like living in a foreign country locked inside America, she embraced that identity, just like her father had.

"He didn't wave the rebel flag around, but my dad was very proud of where he was from. He wanted the world to know, 'I'm a Southern poet, by god,'" she remembers. "I was raised that way, and I like being thought of as a Southerner. It's a pride thing."

What's more, those travels made her comfortable with the kind of constant change that would go on to define much of her life and many of her songs. Her discography is a mercurial, beautiful, and damaged landscape of lovers who enter and exit, places that come in through the windshield and exit through the rearview, feelings that flood and then evaporate. On her second album, 1980's *Happy Woman Blues*, she sang, "I think I lost it, let me know if you come across it / Let me know if I let it fall along a back road somewhere." It's unclear whether she's singing of a love or perhaps satisfaction itself.

The theme winds through her catalog, from 1988's "Passionate Kisses" to 1992's "Sidewalks of the City," from 2001's "Out of Touch" to 2008's "If Wishes Were Horses." When she reprised "I Lost It" for her 1998 breakthrough, *Car Wheels on a Gravel Road*—the album that canonized her within the upper echelon of American songwriters—the move felt less like an attempt to retread a great song and more like a proclamation of continuity: Lucinda Williams songs have forever been seesaws of happiness and sadness, sex and desire, and they probably always will be.

There's an earned toughness there, too. Like her

"Just because I'm married doesn't mean I'm always going to be happy. From the moment of birth, the doctor slaps you, and you cry. That's what life is."

—*Lucinda Williams*

father, Williams initially encountered skepticism about her career choice. She started taking piano lessons before she was a teenager "with this little old guy" whose house was decorated with pink wallpaper and tchotchkes; it was uncomfortable, and she wasn't patient enough for piano, anyway. Miller noticed her interest and, as was the case with so many musicians of her generation, a Silvertone from the Sears catalog became her first guitar. She took lessons with a teacher who showed her how to pick "Puff the Magic Dragon." She began writing; in a family where the written word was sacrosanct, her enthusiasm was nursed along.

Still, during her abbreviated stint at the University of Arkansas, a Spanish teacher told her she should rethink her musical ambitions. Williams never understood why: "Just like when my dad was going to college, there's always that advice they give you, I guess," she deadpans.

Decades later, that same teacher came backstage at a show in Ohio and confessed that she'd been wrong. That admission represented the redemption of another quarter-century struggle for Williams.

Three months shy of his 70th birthday, Tom Southwick admits that his memory is beginning to fade, but he still vividly recalls his first encounter with Williams, as she stood and sang on the back of a flatbed truck in Houston, Texas, a few days after he'd heard her play a few songs on a local radio station. He was recently divorced, living in a furnished two-room apartment ("about as low as you could you go without living in a box by the road"), and was looking for some excitement. He decided to go see her.

"It was November 15, 1975. She was playing a 12-string guitar and singing the Mississippi Delta blues, which was unusual on a 12-string," he remembers. "She was on a truck in the parking lot behind a bookstore. I had never seen anything quite like it: She was an average-sized woman with this big ol' guitar, belting out blues that were 99 percent performed by men. She was playing against the type, and she sang strong and steady. It wasn't a chirpy voice with perfect pitch. She understood the form innately."

Williams had recently relocated from Austin to

Houston after a stint in New Orleans, where she'd sat on a stool in a bar and played four-hour acoustic shifts while sharing an apartment with a topless dancer. Anchored around the legendary venue Anderson Fair, Houston's thriving folk scene offered more opportunities to be heard than Austin or New Orleans. Southwick became a fan, going to almost all of her Houston shows and steadily becoming her confidant.

As Williams began to build area attention, Southwick's own plight also began to improve. He was a single guy and a computer programmer, so he had money to spare. They were both looking for stable housing in Houston, so he invited Williams to live in his large one-bedroom apartment. She took the rectangular laundry room with a window at either end, adding the little desk where she started to write. Southwick refused to let her split the rent.

"I kept saying, 'I need to get a job,' and Tom would say, 'No, don't worry about it. Go play your music. I just want to see you do well,'" Williams says. "He was just a big music fan with no ulterior motives whatsoever."

They lived together for 14 months, a period that proved to be pivotal in both of their lives. At one point, a college friend of Williams', Carol Hunter, visited the pair in Houston. She and Southwick fell for one another, got married, had twins, and later moved to New Jersey together, eventually divorcing in 2005. Williams kept working on new numbers in her little laundry-room apartment, delivering them most anywhere that would have her.

One night she played at a student union building at the University of Houston. The room was crowded, but hardly anyone paid attention. The humbling lack of momentum, in spite of her best efforts, slowly enraged her. At another bar, she played Dylan's epic "Desolation Row" in its entirety. Southwick listened, but few others did. Exasperated, she ran into the rain and yelled, "I hate Houston!"

"I could hardly blame her. I didn't think much of it myself at that point, either," Southwick says. "She wasn't someone who could just sing quietly. She wasn't like a piano player in a restaurant; she had songs to sing, stories to tell. She never felt like she had a choice. This is what she had to do with her life."

Williams had built a reputation in the city's active folk scene, but her constant writing, playing, and socializing took its toll. She developed nodes on her throat and started losing her voice. She eventually returned to Arkansas, moving back in with her father and commu-

nicating for six weeks only by written notes. When she started playing again, she heard from an old friend, a songwriter named Jeff Ampolsk, who told her to reach out to Folkways Records in New York. They'd issued a collection of his jumpy, slight acoustic numbers called *Gods, Guts & Guns*, and he told Williams that they'd put out most anything.

Folkways didn't let her down: They sent her $250, the budget for recording her first album, *Ramblin'*. She cut it in a day in a studio in Jackson, Mississippi, with the help of one of her father's longtime friends. She was still poor, but she had managed to make a record. She decided to follow Ampolsk's other encouragement and make the jump to New York's Greenwich Village, where so many of her heroes, particularly Bob Dylan, had found opportunity.

Back in Houston, Southwick and a consortium of early Williams believers who called themselves G.L.O.H, or Get Lucinda Out of Houston, cobbled together the cash to help her make the trip. In New York, she met Dylan at Gerde's Folk City, and Moses Asch—the legendary and aging founder of her label—in his office. But she despised the city, and after eight months she retreated back to Houston.

Folkways sent her $500 to record her second album, *Happy Woman Blues*. Her father and Southwick pitched in to finance the rest of the recording, done at night and under the radar at a professional studio back in Houston. It wasn't a commercial or critical breakthrough, but those 11 tracks were an epiphany and victory for Williams.

Upon recording her debut, she had assumed that Folkways wasn't interested in some young white woman's thoughts, so she cut a blues disc. "I wasn't really known as a songwriter then, so I was going by what I thought they would want," Williams explains. "I didn't know how many of my songs were good at that time."

But when it came time to record *Happy Woman Blues*, her confidence had blossomed. She had a band and several songs she liked. The record of originals represented the first of Williams' many triumphs over her own assumptions about the music industry and its assumptions about her. *Happy Woman Blues* also signaled the launch of a sad, sweet Southern stylist.

Still, for the better part of the next decade, the music industry spurned Williams. Her talent seemed clear, but no one knew how to market it. Exactly what lured Southwick to her music—this beautiful young woman singing this gritty, stylized mix of old country, rock, and blues as though it was all she knew how to do—confounded record executives. After she moved to Los Angeles in the mid-'80s, major labels started showing up for her sets. She worked shifts in record and book stores; the last day job she remembers is a stint heating up samples of gourmet sausages on a griddle and doling them out to grocery shoppers. She lasted one day.

In 1984, CBS Records gave her a development deal and advanced her a six-month living stipend to write what they hoped would become an album. They passed on the demo, which eventually landed at Rough Trade Records, who weren't concerned about Williams' marketability.

"For big labels, I fell in the cracks between county and rock. There was no Americana back then," she says with a sigh. "Rough Trade were European, they didn't care about that crap."

The Rough Trade album created a buzz that her first two records hadn't; by self-titling it, too, Williams fostered the feeling that she was only now emerging, not reemerging after a decade of relative failure. Major-label interest returned; Bob Buziak, the head of RCA, wanted to sign her. She was reluctant to leave Rough Trade, which had taken a chance on her, but Buziak's "independent spirit" appealed to her. She said yes.

Buziak was soon fired, and Williams was left working with people who didn't know what to do with her. They wanted something they could put on the radio. They wanted big bass and drums and slight vocals, not singer-driven country-rock. Her new label representative began shipping off early recordings for the album that became *Sweet Old World* to be remixed. Each time RCA would get a new track back, she'd walk the six blocks to the office to hear the results.

"I hated it. The A&R guy's jumping up and down in his Gucci shoes, going, 'It's a record! It's a record!'" Williams says. "I didn't want to be there anymore, but they wouldn't let me go."

So Williams, who had become a critical favorite after the Rough Trade album, decided to voice her unhappiness to the industry at large. During a South by Southwest panel about the crossroads of creativity and capitalism, she railroaded RCA, explaining the shuffle of executives who had tried to bend her sound and their unwillingness to let her manage her own musical risks. Word of her unhappiness spread.

"The next day, I get a call from my manager: 'You're dropped.' He was pissed off, but I just said, 'Yes!'" she remembers. "I was so passionate about artist independence. It just took me a long time to find the right people to work with in the studio, men who didn't boss me around and tell me what to do."

Again, the lessons of her father applied: He'd been turned down for several jobs, she says, because he was a "Southern poet," a stigma that implied a certain slowness and provinciality. Her backwater Southern sensibilities presented a roadblock for label executives who wanted a polished product. She wanted everything to have the wild edge of an O'Connor short story or of Dylan's *Highway 61 Revisited*. She had to find others who agreed.

In 1992, Williams finally issued *Sweet Old World* through eclectic indie label Chameleon. Six years later, after a distended and near-disastrous recording process, Mercury released her landmark, *Car Wheels on a Gravel Road*. For its follow-up, 2001's *Essence*, she moved to Lost Highway, a new Americana branch of Universal. It was a comfortable fit and the platform by which Williams became a legitimate roots-music star.

It's hard to imagine what might have happened to Williams had she stuck with RCA and the recordings she has sometimes disparaged as "disco." Maybe she would have become a one-hit wonder, squashing the credibility that she'd spent nearly a quarter-century developing. But she seems too hardscrabble for that fate, too tough to be denied the chance to share her blues. Southwick, the one who helped finance her life in Houston, calls it "her indestructible kind of determination."

After all, Williams emphasizes that at no point did she consider that she might be something *besides* a songwriter, despite all the rejections and strife.

"Something inside me kept pushing me forward. I never had this attitude like, 'I haven't made it yet,'" she says. "I just knew I had this *thing*."

Tom Overby had been in the record business long enough to know that his wife would soon be, once again, without a label. In 2003, Overby moved to Los Angeles to help establish Fontana, the arm of Universal Music Group that distributes titles from independent labels. He'd worked for years as a high-level music buyer at Best Buy before moving on to artist development and marketing at a record label in Nashville. He un-

"I hated it. The A&R guy's jumping up and down in his Gucci shoes, going, 'It's a record! It's a record!'"

—Lucinda Williams

derstood how Music City worked, and, by 2011, he was beginning to understand that Lost Highway, where Williams had been for a decade, had become a lost cause.

Before Williams' fifth album with the label, *Blessed*, could be finished, the layoffs began. Artists began not renewing their contracts. Founder Luke Lewis told Overby and Williams that he would do his best to keep her on the label and to keep the label alive, but if they wanted to pursue other options, he wouldn't begrudge the decision.

Lost Highway released its last record in April 2012, a year after *Blessed* became the fourth consecutive Williams LP to crack the Billboard Top 20. Again, at 60, Williams was an unsigned artist.

Williams tends to talk about the music business like an old friend she stopped liking long ago but to whom, for reasons of necessity, she remains close. "I had no idea where we were going to end up." She and Overby had long toyed with the idea of launching their own imprint, in part to help issue music by old friends who had also been waylaid by a changing industry. As they approached labels with their talks of new music, they made that intention clear. They wanted to start their own home for Williams' music and, if the time was right, put out a record by someone else, too.

Thirty Tigers, a Nashville company in part responsible for the solo rise of former Drive-By Trucker Jason Isbell and the ascendance of Sturgill Simpson, agreed. Williams would retain her own masters and publishing rights, meaning that her takeaway pay could be much

higher. They called the label Highway 20 after the interstate that cuts from Texas through Louisiana, Mississippi, and Georgia—"where I grew up," says Williams.

She and Overby got back to work, meeting with multiple producers, weighing costs and timetables. In the end, they decided to keep the affair cheap, relaxed, and close to their Los Angeles home. They recorded at an old but updated studio named Dave's Home, run by veteran engineer David Bianco. It was a small, intimate room in a working-class section of North Hollywood. The short drive allowed Williams, who sleeps into the early afternoon unless business forces her up earlier, to wake at her leisure. When she arrived each day, the band would be waiting and ready.

Williams notoriously recorded *Car Wheels on a Gravel Road* at least three times before she was satisfied enough to release it. Shortly after Overby first met her, he sat in on her early sessions for *West*. He was stunned when she scrapped the lot of it, electing only to keep her vocals. For *Down Where the Spirit Meets the Bone*, she reversed the perfectionist curse, filling three albums with material in the time she'd allotted for just one record. The bandleader who'd previously been painted as a petulant tyrant who fired people on a whim now calls the group "her little family."

"I was able to get there in the late afternoon. We'd cut a song, take a break and have dinner, cut another song," she says. They took their time, even going on short tours during the sessions so they could work the songs in front of an audience. "It was the best recording experience I've ever had."

Williams had been entertaining the idea of releasing a double album for years, but at Lost Highway, Lewis always led her to reconsider, warning that the cost for fans would simply be too high. Now on her own, she decided to go for it. *Down Where the Spirit Meets the Bone* clocks in at 20 tracks and 100 minutes. The plan paid off, as it is perhaps the broadest and best representation of Williams' talents yet.

It's not all heartbreak, either; she roots for solidarity and social concerns, always taking shots from the position of the underdog. The sashaying "West Memphis," for instance, is a convict ballad turned sociopolitical send-up, where a native Southerner lampoons the same systems from which she rose. During "Everything But the Truth," Williams sprints and stutters through proclamations of self-empowerment and self-improvement over the cocky organ runs of Ian McLagan, in some of the late keyboardist's final sessions.

The coruscating, slow soul number "One More Day" reprises Williams' past as the poet laureate of bad breakups. Alongside weeping horns and moping guitars, she pleads, "Give me one more day / To spend a couple bucks / And place my bet / And win back your love." It's a stunning, subtle rejoinder for those who wondered if she could write sad songs while happily married. Her voice pocked by experience, Williams makes the hurt feel real, like it's her life at that moment, not her life reflected in a moment.

But the actual magic of *Down Where the Spirit Meets the Bone* arrives in its songs of strength and resolve. The crackling "Walk On" is a call for confidence when battling apparently long odds. "Come on, girl, walk on," Williams offers in the refrain, an elder unveiling earned wisdom. She wrote it for her sole goddaughter, the daughter of her long-term boyfriend prior to Overby. She's a good kid, Williams says, a former homecoming queen now going to college outside of Nashville. Williams likes to think she's had a positive impact on her life; at the very least, she wants to offer the kind of encouragement and empowerment that she once found in people like Southwick and her father.

"I don't know how she came out of that situation like she did. She's one of those kids who doesn't want to make the same mistakes her parents made," Williams says. "She hasn't gotten into drugs or drinking. She hasn't gotten pregnant."

During "Protection," which follows Williams' opening rendition of her father's poem, snarling guitars speak to each other in stereo. She packs six decades of experience into five perspicacious minutes: "Well, I've seen some things in life, as God as my witness / I've cried and cried, and nobody could help." By song's end, though, she has emerged as her own biggest champion and defender, employing an economy of words and rhythms that recalls, in passing, her father the poet: "My burden is lifted when I stand up / And use the gift I was given for not givin' up." The band goes quiet during that last line; that's *her* mantra.

Williams laughs when she talks about her life and career and how long it's taken her to reach certain points—a stable marriage, a relationship with a man who inspires her to write, a reputation that no longer requires the imprimatur or aegis of a large corporation.

"It's just worked out that way. It certainly wasn't a conscious effort on my part for things to take that long," Williams says, her warm raspy chuckle coming so hard, quick, and loud that she has to pause for several seconds. "My career has certainly had a mind of its own. It's a little bit of a mystery, I guess—how I ended up where I am, at my age."

In a way, Williams' good humor recalls what she said about her father, how she'd already shed her tears for him by the time he died. Between the deceased lovers and the failed romances, the broken label deals and the divorced friends, the little laundry room bedsit and the dismissed bands, Williams has had plenty to cry about since she wrote "The Wind Blows" on her Silvertone as a teenager. But what's the point of mourning lost time if it helped mold you?

"The fact that it took longer has been better for me. When I was first starting out, I wasn't very advanced as a writer or a singer," she says. "People get it in their heads that, 'If I haven't done *this* by *this* age, I'm just going to quit.' Maybe the difference is that I just went with it. There are no plans. You just have to hang on and ride it out, you know?"

Maybe, then, Lucinda Williams has never been late, even when a crowd of people inside an anxious auditorium wait for her to walk down the aisle. It's just that she is, and has always been, on her own time. ✍

GRAYSON HAVER CURRIN *is a longtime* Pitchfork *contributor.*

PHOTO BY GREG ALLEN

White Lies:

Branson's Ballin' Monoculture

BY LIZ ARMSTRONG

ILLUSTRATIONS BY ELLEN VAN ENGELEN

"I do skin layers," a blonde woman carefully explains. "Six times over in a convection oven."

She was describing the technical process of her new business, a brick-and-mortar addition to a national craze among the intersection of doll and living child aficionados that had just opened on Highway 76 in Branson, Missouri. On this dewy spring morning, it was being advertised from the street by a neon-shirted banjo jamboree. Adults cradling children (very few actually animate) waved to those speeding by, inviting us to stop on in.

Known as the Strip, a portion of this narrow byway is lit up at night like Shanghai during Chinese New Year, bulbs and neon blazing with marquees bearing musical variety performances that consistently bring in an estimated $11 million in tourist revenue. There are 110 different shows this year and, with more seats than Broadway, Branson bills itself as the Live Entertainment Capital of the World.

Inside the store, guests are treated to the blonde woman's creations and their behind-the-scenes: extremely lifelike silicone bundles of joy weighted to feel like real babies, and the paints, brushes, and mohairs that made them who they are today. There's noticeable difference between the Caucasian babies—healthy cheeked, full-lipped, long-eyelashed, chubby, angelic, and at peace, in perfectly crisp white socks and gleamingly clean new clothes—and the others, which look more like dolls. Those with the darkest skin are dressed in ill-fitting clothing made from rags, hair frizzed and wild, expressions humble, shrieking, or proudly flipping up a hand. They look hard, angry, embarrassed, painted beyond caricature. A collectible to commemorate latent racism rather than a surrogate for love.

Branson is a town of contradiction—an odd combination of unbearable innocence, kitschy glam, pristine nature, sharky business maneuvers, World War II–era Christian family values, and silent struggle. Despite impressive stats, the local economy has seen a consistent decline in tourism, but most visitors wouldn't know it from the hairspray, rhinestones, and perma-smiles. The royal quadrumvirate of family, faith, patriotism, and spectacle dance together in a performance that shuts out the area's meth problem, financial issues, gay population, self-awareness, and all the rest of the world too.

Up until the 1960s, Highway 76 was just another country highway. In 1959 the Mabe family moved down from Springfield and started a bluegrass family revue that included handmade instruments, one crafted from a mule's jawbone. The Baldknobbers, as they called their act, performed on the lakefront to fishermen. Then along came the Presleys, another family from Springfield, who since the early 1940s had been touring all around the Ozarks on flatbed trucks and in caves, which had bad acoustics but natural air conditioning in sweltering summers. They opened the very first musical theater on Highway 76 with a three-generation act called the Presleys' [sic] Country Jamboree, and Branson history was forever changed.

Hee Haw co-host and famous country musician Roy Clark caught wind of Branson—other country stars like Dolly Parton, Buck Trent, and Porter Wagoner had been coming to town to perform since the '70s—and in 1983 became the first celebrity to own and operate his own theater there. Boxcar Willie put down Branson roots in 1987, the same year a Japanese fiddler named Shoji, who'd already earned his stripes in the Grand Ole Opry, opened what is still considered one of the most elaborate theaters on the Strip. His men's and women's lounges were inducted in the Restroom Hall of Fame, with marble fireplaces, onyx sinks, real gold leafing, billiards tables, and other fixtures and antiques from around the world.

By the time country funnyman Ray Stevens opened his 2,000-seat theater in 1991, 4 million visitors were pouring into the 22 independently owned theaters annually. That year, *60 Minutes* did a segment on Bran-

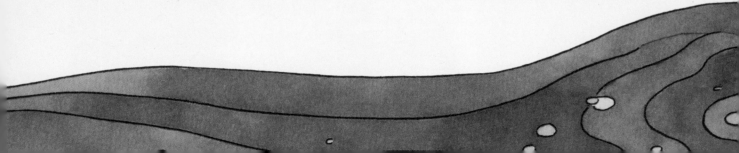

son where Roy Clark bragged about the billion-and-a-half dollar revenue the Strip was pulling in. It wasn't quite true, but that hyperbole—along with images of folks praying over cheap, heaping plates of food—quickly turned Branson into a retirement town for country ballers.

One after another they came and placed their stake in the ground: Andy Williams, Jim Stafford, Tony Orlando, Wayne Newton, Kenny Rogers—all the country stars of yore kept coming, each opening his own theater with no promoters, no producers, no agents. Then came the Lennon Sisters (and brothers) with the Lawrence Welk Band, and New York comedian Yakov Smirnoff, whose patriotic immigrant character played well to Branson audiences.

Touring and hustling was fine for all these people back when they were younger, but who wants to be 50 and on the road 200 days a year? Here, performers were sole proprietors of their own enterprises and got to sleep in the same bed every night.

Within 25 years, with its lakes, ancient caves, outlet shopping, a 19th-century mining-town-themed amusement park, and a two-lane highway of non-stop musical entertainment blazing with neon flourishes and flamboyant architectural oddities, Branson had become a vacationing haven for the middle of the United States. Those who love their country, love their nature, love their beef, love their Jesus, and love their show tunes still flock to Branson in arthritic herds. It's the Las Vegas of the Bible Belt.

I'd been invited to Branson for the town premiere of *We Always Lie to Strangers*, a documentary film about local culture co-directed by AJ Schnack and an old friend of mine, David Wilson. In 2003 Wilson co-founded the documentary-specific True/False Film Festival in Columbia, Missouri, which boosted a vibrant yet economically depressed art scene. He'd become a town hero and something of a tastemaker, too.

We caught up on our lives, relationships, and cooking expertise while strolling through the Landing, an outdoor mall and walkway along the Taneycomo lakefront, with the usual touristy things like margarita bars, photo booths, piped-in music, and a store that sells only different flavors of olive oil. We decided we'd come back later and try out the hurricane booth, where for a few bucks you can hop into a clear plastic vestibule that fills itself with high-powered wind and experience the terror of a natural disaster while everyone around you watches.

"Gail, what's the deal with Jim Stafford?" an elderly man asks. "I'll find out through the grapevine," Gail sasses. Upon her next return from the kitchen, she reports that he's now in Florida. "He got divorced." The rest of the conversation comes in snippets: "2008..." "four to six months..." "condo..." "gated." A local news story would break a few months later that told of Jim Stafford's defaulted loan on his extravagant theater (shows included laser lights *and* Chihuahuas) of which he still owed close to $2 million. Allegedly.

On our way to Silver Dollar City—a religious-mining-town–themed amusement park—we drive through the Strip, quiet and slightly ramshackle in daylight. It's hard to tell what's been abandoned or shut down and what's just inactive when the sun is out. Twenty years ago Branson was expanding so fast it couldn't manage its sewage. Now, according to a marketing report from the Branson/Lakes Area Chamber of Commerce, it's shrinking. The town seems to have climbed to its apex in 2007, when it drew more than 8 million visitors, but tourism's been on the decline ever since.

We glide over lush green hills, through dense forests of oak and dogwood, stopping off at Table Rock Lake, formed when the United States Army Corps of Engineers dammed the White River in 1958 for flood control and hydroelectric purposes. Despite nearby commercial developments—among them a zipline, showboat, and racetrack—pristine panoramas of the bluffs harken back to times when progress was measured in ice ages.

Silver Dollar City was exactly what you would expect from a deeply conservative, faux-19th-century Midwestern theme park: a mixture of hilarity, sadness, fried pork skins, white leather geriatric sneakers, bland expressions, and role-playing at all levels of internal awareness.

Wilson and I took a magical walking tour through the mammoth onsite Marvel Cave, a living womb sparkling with waterfalls in narrow corridors, long believed by indigenous people and early explorers alike to be the actual mouth of Hades. We toured all the old-timey stuff too: a blacksmith, apple butter chefs, potters, candy pullers, glass blowers, a butcher, a baker, a candle-stick maker... I learned to play the mountain dulcimer from a gentleman in a vest who became increasingly frustrated with my refusal to play perfectly harmonic successive chords.

Silver Dollar City is a cliché that is delightful in its campiness, depressive in its fan base, enraging in its sexist gender stereotyping, and utterly stifling to anyone traveling from a more cosmopolitan area. It's a slice of America that most coastal folk prefer to avoid.

It's an intellectual challenge to step into a place where the values skew wildly right from one's own, like having Thanksgiving dinner with racist grandparents who feel justified in hanging on to their values because "that's just the way things were when I was growing up." No matter how open-minded we city folk think we are, we always visit these parks and parts of the country with a smirking sort of shock and a self-righteous point of view. *Wow, people think shit like this is fun?* The thought runs on a feedback loop, building an anthropologically fascinating soufflé of observation, until it just collapses in tired resignation.

"Branson attractions mediate a set of essential 'down-home' values that attract 'pilgrims' to a set of sacred ideas," writes academic researcher Aaron Ketchell in his elucidating *Holy Hills of the Ozarks: Religion and Tourism in Branson, Missouri*. He explores Branson's curiously tepid blend of Christianity and recreation, how the city became a mecca of conservative Christianity—a place for "spiritual vacation"—through rigor-

ously enforced ideals. "Nothing that would offend your grandma," goes the popular saying in town. And you'd better be going to church on Sundays.

Branson's currency for success is measured not just in dollars but also in the precision of one's moral compass. Foul language onstage, for instance, would drive a show immediately bankrupt. Cleavage is unseemly and unacceptable. The issue with calibration of this sort, however, is that it assumes there is one true north, when in fact—when it comes to human ethics and behavior and culture—it's all a matter of perception.

In Branson, the ones doing the perceiving are decidedly white and old. As reported in the 2010 census, Branson's racial composition was 89 percent White, 8.8 percent Hispanic or Latino, 2 percent African American, 1.5 percent Asian, and 0.9 percent Native American. Nearly half of the population was at least 45 years of age.

The importance of racial diversity is quietly trivialized, or unacknowledged at best; this is evidenced not only in the latest craze in dolls, but also in Dolly Parton's Dueling Dixie Stampede. For this rodeo dinner theater on horseback, spectators are split between North and South as they cheer for their respective sides in a competitive equine obstacle course evoking the Civil War. "Some nights," Wilson tells me, "the South wins."

In terms of Outfitters, Branson's is Dixie rather than Urban—and they operate in a chain, selling confederate memorabilia. "But that's super marginal out here," Wilson says as we pass it, in a strip mall next to the Jerky Outlet. In the proper South, for better or worse, the whole Dixie thing is all over the place. But Missouri isn't the South—not quite.

Missouri has a history of repressed turmoil, starting in 1821 with its inclusion into the Union. Statehood had been steadily growing ever since Delaware kicked it all off in 1787. Missouri's territory was included in the Louisiana Purchase, but getting its own star on the flag was such a crazy traumatizing mess that

Silver Dollar City was exactly what you would expect from a deeply conservative, faux–19th–century Midwestern theme park: a mixture of hilarity, sadness, fried pork skins, white leather geriatric sneakers, bland expressions, and role–playing at all levels of internal awareness.

other states weren't incorporated for another 16 years.

In its inception, Missouri had petitioned for slave status, which, when granted, would throw off the whole 50/50 balance of free states versus not. So the white-hairs running the show threw in a sovereign Maine to keep the tension symmetrically rife. After it was ruled that Missouri was to be the only state north of the 36°30' latitude line (note: not the Mason Dixon) that allowed slavery, Thomas Jefferson had a psychic flash that this would be the death of the "united" part of the new country's name. And he was right. Known as the

Missouri Compromise, it either abated the Civil War for forty years, or fueled it—depending on whom you ask.

Adding Missouri as a slave state meant that Congress officially condoned the expansion of human abuse for capital gains, but not everyone in the nation was down for that. In fact, Missouri residents wanted it both ways, and no one could ever tell who stood for what—the only indicator being who was working in one's fields. Hence its wary motto: "The Show Me State."

When the Civil War hit, Missouri became a state of "armed neutrality," complete with a pro-Confederate

In Branson, what you see is what you get.

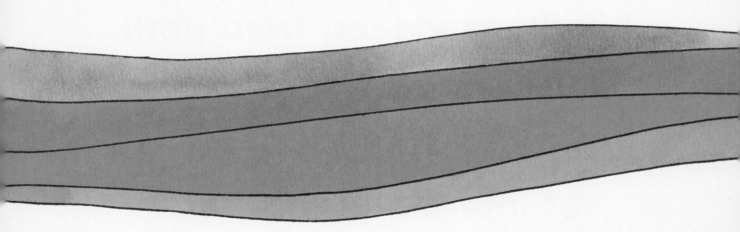

militia to fight against whatever it wanted. But since the state was divided—even within its own government—this was a recipe for disaster, and Missouri was inundated with vicious neighbor-on-neighbor guerilla warfare. Was this legit military action, or was this pure crime? No one could really tell, which only further inflamed what was already a lawless blur of a state.

Needless to say, there was a lot of unresolved bullshit after the war, including this hate-filled "bushwhacker" fighting. These tactics birthed some ultrafamous outlaws there, including Jesse James and his crew. Marauding gang activity started trending, and it infiltrated the state.

Branson is located in Taney County, which, despite a relatively low population of slaves before the war compared to other slave-holding counties in Missouri, was

still legislatively and judiciously corrupt. Government leaders had been bought and elected by these outlaw gangs, and as a result, in the 20 years after the war not a single suspect was ever convicted of murder, despite plenty of killing going on.

Eventually, enough was enough. In 1883 a small army of hillbilly vigilantes banded together in protest of the local government and authorities, determined to enforce the law themselves. They met up in the stark Ozark Mountains and planned their revenge. Unfortunately, as the mountains were basically just glorified hills in size and sparsely vegetative (aka the "bald knobs"), everyone could see these guys conspiring. However, no one imagined they'd come screaming down into town wearing crazy scary horned hoods and truly take care of all the problems the cops couldn't handle.

First up was breaking into the Taney County jail to free their roughneck buddies. The Bald Knobbers (as the terrified townspeople called them) intended to seek justice but ended up corrupting it further, diminishing in ethics as they grew in size—publicly beating, whipping, branding, or straight-up killing anyone they thought deserved it. Five years after they started, their leader was assassinated. By 1899, it was over.

Branson was founded—though not yet incorporated—in 1903, intended for logging. A railway was being built, and they needed timber for the track. So they had a mini logging industry for a second, but after that was over not much else grew out there. Rich, deep soil couldn't gain traction on the steep hillsides, and everywhere else regularly flooded. Settlers had already made weird attempts to build local economies: lead and marble mining in caves filled with nothing but guano, or collecting mussel shells from riverbeds for the button industry.

In 1907, bestselling Victorian (and mega-Christian) author Harold Bell Wright—a sort of V.C. Andrews of Ozarkian premodernism nostalgia—initially put Branson on the map with a byzantine hillfolk dramatic novel called *The Shepherd of the Hills*. The book was a national bestseller, and a newly completed rail line unleashed a flood of tourism and culture to a part of the world that had been a hinterland for so long. It seems insane that a settler-period religious drama could set the nation aflame, but this story resonated like the Bible itself, exposing the fruits and losses of the Manifest Destiny generation. Four films stemmed from the book, as did an outdoor play staged in Bran-

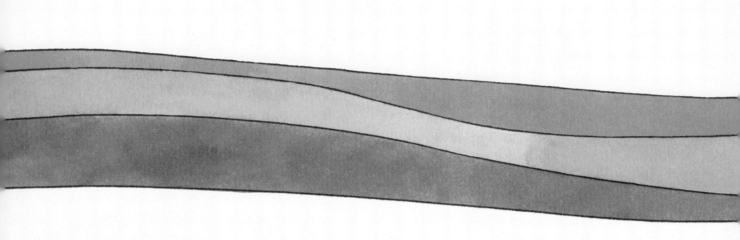

son for five months of the year from 1960 to 2013 (it's back on periodically now, too).

In retrospect, the town seemed destined for tourism, as it really couldn't sustain any other industry. It was incorporated in 1912 and became an official vacation destination a couple years later, with new attention focused on its lake scene: boating and splashing and general aqueous cheer. Despite all the attention, however, its hill population closely guarded their practices and stories, rarely letting the outside in or the inside out.

Preeminent Branson folklorist Vance Randolph calls the people of this area "deliberately unprogressive." They've stuck resolutely to their practices for the last hundred-some years, he says, ideas that were "developed" by pioneers who came west from southern Appalachia.

For decades Randolph carefully studied this frozen-in-time clandestine culture, living in the environment he was documenting, drinking and fishing and pissing outside just like everybody else. Indefatigable, he wrote more than a dozen books on Ozark folklore and was widely recognized for his immersive academic approach. It's what got him to *We Always Lie to Strangers*, a collection of tall tales that dissects the particular finesse of storytelling while practicing it too. In the story for which the book was named, the punch line explains it all: just like the Devil himself, no one in the Ozarks makes a practice of telling the whole truth.

Perhaps that's why Wilson and Schnack had to spend five years there in order to make any sense of it at all for their film. They'd initially headed into Branson in November 2007 in hopes of finding a secret music scene. With so much talent concentrated in one area, they figured, surely these people were forming bands aside from their variety show fare, letting it rip on open mics or behind the scenes. Surely they weren't all totally serious about this bluegrass-and-country, Jesus-and-heteronormativity-*only* policy, right?

The answer was no. In Branson, what you see is what you get.

Between 2007 and 2012, Wilson and Schnack moved into Branson for months at a time, following several musical acts—often people related by blood or connected through romance—through different phases of their careers. It was contemporary folkloric immersion of a Randolphic order, and their hope was to grab some truth after watching so much staged performance.

Eventually they settled on five families, ranging from the now well-oiled machine of the Presleys to a group of folks creating and launching their first big show on the Strip. The closer Wilson and Schnack looked, the more they realized how a practice of lying to strangers meant covering up economic struggle and a gay population—things that more cosmopolitan areas of the United States take for granted. We're used to glamour and glitz and showmanship serving as key indicators of advancement, enlightenment, or open-mindedness. In Branson, it's the exact opposite.

Just like the book for which their film was named, an outsider would never see the whole picture.

The morning *We Always Lie to Strangers* is to be screened in town for the first time, I wake up to a printed letter slipped under my door, warning me, as a valued guest, of a severe weather advisory. "In case a tornado warning is issued for Taney County," it reads, "close your blackout drapes and take cover in your bathroom. In the event a tornado does strike the hotel, your guest room bathroom is the safest area."

The storm started during our champagne brunch at the historic Worman House, which is about as elegant and grandiose as a hunting-lodge-cum-manse gets. Surrounded by stained glass, pristine woodwork, and extreme taxidermy (a grizzly guards the ladies' room), guests are treated to a world-class breakfast buffet in the middle of the woods. In a large private room with panoramic windows, Schnack and Wilson, Bill and Gail Lennon, the film's producers, the town's tourism board, and I toasted to Branson while we watched the black clouds roll in.

Evening comes quick. Two whole theaters fill up in the multiplex, with more people waiting to get into the screening. Nearly 400 of us altogether watch a story of how a small town white-knuckles its values, tightens its chops, and makes a go of it. Because showmanship in Branson is not just about getting onstage and dazzling 'em all, it's also small-business entrepreneurship.

We see how a startup outfit increasingly devalues itself in hopes of greater ticket sales, growing from hopeful to jaded. The defeat through the smiles and rhinestones, the bodies dancing, stiff from stress. How tirelessly these performers—and all the rest—promote themselves all day, donning full faces of makeup in the woods or at an air show to project an image of stardom to the public at all times. At night, they struggle to find childcare so they can put on their costumes and exhaust themselves artistically, then clean the theater's toilets afterward. Morale plummets as in-fighting escalates, gossip you wouldn't expect to hear this side of seventh grade becomes the sole mode of communication, and fear for security and livelihood is taken to *Game of Thrones*–levels of survival.

We see how the Lennon Sisters (first made famous in Venice, California, for 13 years of performances on the iconically wholesome *Lawrence Welk Show*, beginning in 1955) continue to perform for decades in Branson as their fan base becomes too old to come to the theater, mining their own willpower for creativity. How their brother Bill and his wife Gail dare erect an independent 1940s-style jazz and ragtime revue, the former appearing regularly on the radio as the town's loudest liberal Democrat.

We see Chip, a performer who is beautiful, chiseled, and gay; he's sort of out in the world, but not to his children. When the film begins, he's in a new relationship with a man. They'll go on dates, but he says, "We're not going to walk through the Landing holding hands and make the public uncomfortable."

This film is, among other things, a story of denial, and it implies that there are a lot of other Chips out there. Branson has answers for *what is* but not *why*. There's a nearly deplorable lack of curiosity and an oxymoronic definition of kindness. Change here must come as a force of nature, rather than willful acceptance. And this film might be just that—not a tornado like Branson is used to, whipping up counterculture values and points of view into a destructive funnel that mows down a community. Instead, it's a small earthquake, its collateral damage defined in aftershock.

No one claps afterward; most simply file out of the theater, apparently unaware that it's a special treat when the makers of the film you just watched stick around for a Q&A. Especially when they're also wearing custom-made rhinestone-encrusted red, white, and blue cowboy blazers. I stand outside the doorways of the theaters like a film trailer producer from the '90s, hoping to catch sound-bite reactions from the audience.

No luck. I hit the restroom, where I spy an elderly woman drying her hands—she seems elegant and well-mannered. When I step outside, I spot her with her husband, who I discover after a short amount of small talk is a former pastor. What did they think of the film? "I just didn't agree with some of the language," she says. Saying "fuck" in Branson is like shooting up a child with heroin—it's totally unthinkable. One woman in the film uses the word approximately three times a sentence. "Or his lifestyle," she continues.

My blood freezes. "What do you not agree with?" I ask.

"Well, this is a place you can bring anyone and they won't be offended," she responds. "That man..."

I think for a second, and carefully reply. "Actually, I'm offended," I say. "I'm gay. My partner is a woman, and we're in love."

I register her eyes move from friendly to slightly hostile—a bit startled. She gives me the up-and-down, looking for what public lesbian signals she might have missed. Her husband steps in to try to rescue the situation.

"My granddaughter has those tendencies too, so I'm not blind to it," he says. "But I don't like it. That's just what I was raised with. That's not family values."

"You might want to try simply loving your granddaughter," I tell them. "She probably would appreciate that."

They nod and pleasantly bid me goodnight. I head upstairs to the after-party where I see Chip, now elevated to heroic status in my mind for what he's clearly dealt with for many years. I just start bawling.

Dreams aren't enough in Branson. You need talent, business acumen, and the tenacity to continue with each day the same as all the others, on repeat, until you die. You need the courage to hide who you really are or to readily inhabit the role of mascot, or else to conform like everyone else.

The people we see in *We Always Lie to Strangers* aren't the type who couldn't make it anywhere else. They are people with a very specific vision involving access to beautiful land, a certain quality of life, the ability to support and spend time with their families, and the desire to wear a shitload of fringe and rhinestones.

When people come to Branson for a weekend now, they take in maybe one variety show in a building that hosts three acts a day, and then head to a lake or go shopping, golf, or visit the Butterfly Palace or the Titanic Museum. It's not like people come only to gorge on live entertainment designed in the early '90s to occupy senior citizens.

Over and over again, I hear people talk about Branson having been "built on a World War II model." These were the folks happy to travel on a bus tour, get some shopping done, take in a show, then go to bed happy after saying their prayers. But now people like to drive themselves. They want choices, variety, autonomy on their vacations. The baby boomers changed Branson, and as crazy as it is to be talking about that particular generation as arbiters of change, Branson has been running on a treadmill for decades. No one realized this town would actually become a living history of how musical entertainment as an experience changes.

Building after building has been shutting down. Yakov Smirnoff is back on tour. Shoji isn't doing as many shows. And there's the whole Jim Stafford debacle. Branson's seen a slew of complicated lawsuits against theaters, their owners, developers, banks, and

They look like a combination of cruise ship director, Ronald McDonald, and matador.

the FDIC; money has changed hands fast and visions of fame have crashed.

The Presleys have become the ultimate case study of what it takes to make it on the Strip: fifty years of hard work from music maestros who also got their business degrees, family dynamics that come off as completely loving at all times, TV station ownership, and marriage to the mayor.

Gail Lennon, who sang in a swing music show with her husband Bill and his brother at the Welk Theatre from 1994 to 2004, was hired by Welk's musical heirs, and paid by them too. Separate from Welk, but "part of the Welk galaxy of stars." So when the Welk Show "gave up" on Branson and left, the Lennons were without a contract. The theater remained but there was no one to run it, so the Lennons suddenly had to do everything themselves.

Their show had busloads of tourists already booked by the dozens, but nowhere to stage it. "So we did a partial season at a different theatre," Gail says. "Then a six-week Christmas show with Mickey Rooney. And when Andy Williams got sick, we were brought in to finish out his season. And then again for the Christmas show after he died."

Ultimately, their show didn't survive. Too much hustle, not enough infrastructure. This is not a special scenario in Branson. "That's why the Presleys are so impressive," Gail says. "They don't have to infect themselves."

Nearly every night (except Sundays, of course) from mid-March to mid-December for almost 50 years, the Presleys have put on a show in the same theater—four generations' worth of hillbilly hijinks,

country, gospel, and bluegrass. The night I'm there, the opening number features costumed performers so flamboyant that I can't concentrate on their heads long enough to count the actual number of people singin' and twangin'—each one displaying an ultra-expressive, pleasantly "surprised" showbiz face. Tune after tune, the stage is a blaze of hyper-specific regional fashion: matching rhinestone-studded suits emblazoned with a pattern of fleur-de-lis, red patent leather shoes. They look like a combination of cruise ship director, Ronald McDonald, and matador. It's awesome and beyond intense.

In between the songs about heterosexual marriage, God, and country, a father-son hillbilly clown duo known as Herkimer (the witty and gifted guitarist patriarch in sequined overalls) and Cecil (sort of like an existential country bumpkin Pee-wee Herman) put on little skits, poking fun at each other and the liberals, who are apparently not in this audience. Herkimer teases single, lonely, hopelessly nerdy Cecil, exclaiming, "He's so lonely he shaved one leg so he can feel like he's settin' next to a girl!" Everyone busts up laughing, but it's the anti-Obama joke (which I didn't even understand) that gets the biggest response.

Women get the spotlight here and there, but they're mostly backup singers, decoration, confetti. When one does take the mic herself, she sings us the lament of a girl chasing fame in a big city and regretting it.

The interlude feels like a Pentecostal church sermon, introducing each of the band members and guests by their first names. Of the few female backup singers, only one is introduced by any sort of title, and it's "my wife."

It gets really preachy in the second half, which seems to flood the audience with endorphins. Singing about the blood of the Lord and Jesus as a lighthouse in the rocky sea of life gets silver-haired heads sway-

ing. "You can praise the pain away," a smooth baritone croons in a song that I'm pretty sure is about end-of-life proceedings. This is hospice glam.

At the end of the show the performers invite all the veterans in the house to stand up. Many gentlemen rise, removing their hats and holding them over their hearts. The Presleys launch into a glittering, wet-eyed, fully bellowed "Star-Spangled Banner," saluting these men and women. The rest of the audience stands too. Then the curtain drops.

It feels like I've somehow missed a holiday. "No," Wilson tells me after the show. "Every single performance on the Strip ends with the National Anthem."

After 36 hours in Branson, immediately after the Presleys' Country Jubilee (that strange apostrophe drives me crazy too), I'm really hungry. I haven't eaten much; I live in Los Angeles and eat like it too, and can't find much that's green. Out of hanger, I complain about this to Mayor Raeanne Presley, who has been graciously available throughout my stay, and ask where I can go. It's all steakhouses and buffets as far as I can see down the Strip, but I'm desperate enough to start walking anyway. I make a plan to catch up with Wilson later.

I see the familiar signage curve of a Taco Bell, the road-tripping vegetarian's safe house, and began to hot-step it. Mayor Presley and her husband pull up in their car next to me, not wanting to let a visitor grumble and wander around on her own, and drive me the rest of the way.

Over my meal, we talk about a lot of things, including family, roots, and the show. Mayor Presley is interested, sassy, and not budging on her own opinions in the slightest. It's exactly the way you wish all politicians would be—reasonable yet resolute, transparent, charismatic, human, and deeply invested in the people they're governing—even if you're freaked out by their openly conservative politics and Jesus talk.

I tell them it was fun watching people do what they love, because it was. They're clearly very technically talented and well rehearsed, and you'd have to be a real miser not to enjoy someone's hard work and expression of joy. But I can't help myself—I have to ask why the women are so diminished onstage. Mayor Presley responds clearly and automatically as if I'd asked her the color of the sky. "It's because the women run the business," she says.

Keeping women behind the scenes has been tradition in their family since the inception of the show, starting with Bessie Mae Garrison, who married founding father Lloyd Presley in 1942. Together, she and another woman who married into the family took on work fit for several employees. This included accounting, bills, HR, training, concession stand maintenance. Bessie Mae sewed all the costumes, kept another full-time job, and raised two kids. Pat sold tickets, greeted bus tours, worked with the Branson Chamber of Commerce, ran the gift shop, and troubleshot anything going wrong while the show was running.

Even Mayor Presley does "women's work," helping out with group tours. Her daughter, Sarah, who once played saxophone and fiddle in the Jubilee but decided she didn't like performing, now helps run front of house.

Later, Wilson, Schnack, and I head out with Sarah and some of the other young Presleys to a barroom so full of black light and Skrillex that we have to sit outside. The usual face-pierced kids in low-waist jeans alternate between grinding on one another and playing pool. An elderly couple dressed in exact matching white button-down shirts and khakis sip cocktails at the bar. A few single guys lurk.

The Presleys are town royalty and the bartender comes out to talk. They swap stories about shady developers in town who promised to open up such-and-such but ended up swiping all the cash and splitting.

Nothing comes from nothing. The terrain of the Ozarks is ancient and unmoving, one of the oldest landmasses in the entire world. It's been eroding very slowly since the beginning of time, averse to change since it first peeked its igneous crust out of a vast ocean. Everywhere else on the planet, life was beginning to commit serious marine transgression, but not here. The trilobites and brachiopods, the mollusks and the fish, they all preferred frolicking in the shallow continental seas to growing vestigial parts that would—some scientists say—over many ages allow these evolved creatures to eventually walk and breathe on land.

As the millions of years passed like mayfly lifespans and the continent we would eventually call North America continued to expand westward, portions of this land mass would come up for air only to resubmerge themselves, not quite ready for their destiny as terra firma. Yet as tectonic and geological upheaval and catastrophe alike pummeled its westernmost lip, the land mass stood strong, finding fulfillment as the verdant plateau we now call the Ozark Mountains.

As a parcel of Earth, this area has been anti-evolution since its very beginnings. Maybe somehow its settlers sensed this, allowing God to thoroughly bless the oak, the crooked streams, the pine, the crystal rivers, the ancient caves, and the hills before seizing the land from the provident and peaceful Osage tribe.

Branson has always been defined by its fronts rather than its truths. These shows mean the visitors outnumber the residents 640 to 1. It's ancient territory, as old as God, having been worn down through time, literally changing mountains into molehills, yet its monoculture refuses to change itself.

Branson's industry is new and its land is old, its stories to the world at large conscientiously imbued with half-truths. The lies the town tells sometimes make it a stranger even to itself.

"This place is so unexplainable," Jim Stafford told a *Chicago Tribune* reporter in a 1993 story about Branson's boom. "I believe an awful lot of people have a nagging anxiety that they're going to wake up and nobody's going to be here." ✎

LIZ ARMSTRONG *is an editor and journalist in Los Angeles, and a former Missouri resident.*

Lizzy Mercier Descloux: Behind the Muse

Can you be a trailblazer if you leave no trail?

BY LAURA SNAPES

PHOTOS BY ADAM KIDRON

JOHANNESBURG, 1983

"I will not stay in one place."

—LMD

Lizzy Mercier Descloux died in obscurity in April 2004, 20 years after what was ostensibly her musical heyday. A Lyon-born art school dropout and devotee of Rimbaud and Godard, she was every bit the romantic French archetype, as well as an innovator and witness to numerous pivotal moments in musical and cultural history.

She saw Patti Smith and Television at CBGBs and Basquiat at the Kitchen. She recorded at Compass Point Studios in Nassau while Grace Jones made *Nightclubbing* next door. She collaborated with Soweto musicians in apartheid-era South Africa years before *Graceland*. She persuaded Chet Baker to play trumpet on her penultimate album, which turned out to be one of his final recordings. Though her entire discography has been reissued twice in the 11 years since her death, she has mostly remained a footnote to other people's careers.

In his 2013 autobiography, *I Dreamed I Was a Very Clean Tramp*, Descloux's former lover Richard Hell invokes her memory with grim fetishization ("She was an intellectual sex-kitten chanteuse adventuress little girl"). Most of her old paramours *still* bitch about their rivals' *dreadful* influences on Descloux's career, each claiming a different account of how she *truly* felt and how much control she wielded. Stories abound of various collaborators pushing her in this direction and that while she griped about being worked so hard, yet she freely made five albums and one EP, followed her whims across the globe, and never conveyed anything less than a steely sense of autonomy, engagement, and intent in the many interviews she did during that period.

If there is a conclusive riposte to whether she was mused and used by the men around her, it's in the consistency of her work over that decade—as suitors came and went—which defines her as a visionary, forging unconventional marriages of sound and attempting to push her singing to non-verbal transcendence. When examining Descloux's unique voice, her strong and ever-shifting image, and her considerable achievements, one question becomes immediate: How could such a person possibly have been forgotten by history?

For one night in Paris, on July 8, 2004, Patti Smith elevated Descloux to her rightful stature as a French musical institution. Smith's name was above the door at the venue Le Bataclan in the 11th arrondissement, but her stage backdrop bore Descloux's name and the dates of her life: "1956–2004." During the concert, Smith dedicated "Easter" to her old friend, who had died a few months before, after being diagnosed with cancer the previous year.

In 1978 Smith released "Easter" and the album of the same name, both of which heavily referenced the life of Arthur Rimbaud. A year earlier, she and Descloux had made a more lighthearted tribute to the French poet: A set of photos from 1977 depict Descloux suited up as Rimbaud and Smith in a white dress playing his sister, Isabelle. They dangle off one another like besotted young female friends do, capering around the Soho loft decorated with Soviet flags and Sex Pistols iconography that they shared when Descloux moved from Paris to New York in 1977 to start her musical career.

Smith had arguably introduced Rimbaud to New York's burgeoning punk scene a few years earlier—his dissolute artistic self-sacrifice making him a natural punk godfather—and in Descloux, Smith found someone equally interested in, as Greil Marcus put it in *Lipstick Traces*, "[destroying] the line in favor of the word." At the end of 1977, Descloux made her first release, a book of poetry and collage called *Desiderata*, in which she began pursuing her delight in the rhythmic, nonsensical potential of sound. "I will not stay in one place," she wrote in the untitled French poem that opens the collection. Then, several lines later: "The 'bourgeoisie' is an invention / To kill the weapon of my soul."

Descloux's final recorded output was a bilingual recitation of Rimbaud's "Matinée d'Ivresse" with Smith in 1995 for composer Bill Laswell. Both women sound notably older: Smith's voice is a scathing scrape, while lifelong chainsmoker Descloux has dropped several octaves and smoulders seductively. Although they had lost touch in the intervening years, one line felt like the perfect summation of their late-'70s friendship: "We know how to give our life fully every day," they intone, palimpsest-style.

Descloux got her cultural awakening thanks to another forgotten French musical institution. In 1972, 21-year-old Michel Esteban rented a store for his mail-order rock merchandising company Harry Cover at 12 Rue des Halles, in a working-class neighborhood of Paris. It became the place to go: Kids would convene around the free jukebox, while Malcolm McLaren would visit to keep up with *les branchés*.

Across the road at 11 Rue des Halles lived Descloux with her aunt and uncle. (Her mother wasn't interested in children and her father didn't know she existed until she found him online and met him a few months before her death.[1])

In spring 1975, Esteban spotted the 18-year-old Descloux on the balcony of her aunt and uncle's apartment. Enchanted, he left a note tied to her bike, and she came into his shop. Disillusioned with school and barely showing up for her classes at L'Ecole des Beaux Arts, she dropped out completely after falling in love and moving in with Esteban.

The success of Harry Cover had enabled Esteban to start visiting America, and on a trip to New York in 1974 he befriended the Ramones, Television, and Patti Smith. "I knew something was really happening there," he says. "Nobody was saying anything in the French press, so I thought, why not make a magazine?" He and Descloux started *Rock News* in January 1976; the first issue featured Iggy Pop on the cover, and they distributed 10,000 copies nationwide. After the magazine's launch, the pair continued to make frequent reporting trips to the United States.

Although Descloux described her journalistic endeavors as "completely crap" to a Belgian weekly in 1984, her observations and prose in *Rock News* were unquestionably sharp. On Patti Smith: "Women are usually groupies or the silent circle of photographers, managers, or the soul sister of rock'n'roll. The myth of the sexy pin-up, unthinkable regarding Patti, has been crushed beneath the foot of this strange, neurotic person, who is possessed of a sexual power as unknowable as it is vast." Describing the Sex Pistols: "My kingdom for a vibrator! What is bad taste? That's what the Sex Pistols are asking you. *Alors!* The hugeness of their destitution and the coldness of their boredom freeze our bones in the prime of life."

A mere six months after starting *Rock News*, Esteban and Descloux had already appeared in Amos Poe's documentary *Blank Generation* and commissioned Kim Fowley to interview the Runaways—but then they declared punk dead and closed the magazine. A year later, the couple moved to New York, where Esteban partnered with Michael Zilkha to start the pivotal no wave label ZE Records, and Descloux acquired a Fender Jazzmaster. The couple split up, pledging to keep things strictly business.

Descloux explained, "Once I found myself with a guitar in my hands it was inevitable—I was committed to singing [...] It's easier for me to convey something in song than in writing." Having never played a note before, she embraced her amateur aesthetic (perhaps especially its Rimbaudian rejection of convention?) but remained acutely aware of rock's transcendent potential hidden beneath the prevailing hoary old tropes. Similarly, she told *Creem*, "Very often now when a woman plays guitar they really try to be equal to men, so they're just gonna practice so they sound like Jimmy Page. I think women have a certain sensibility that could make them approach guitar in a very, very different way, in a beautiful way."

"Beautiful" is not quite the word for the approach she took in Rosa Yemen, the duo she formed with Esteban's brother Didier in 1978. She explained the band's two-guitar lineup in an interview with *New York Rocker*: "We couldn't get a drummer—all the drummers we were auditioning, they were almost *scared* of the music [...] It was just too weird." They started playing ferocious shows at clubs like the Kitchen, the murderous intent of their namesakes (European anarchists like Rosa Luxembourg and Germany's Baader Meinhof Group) echoed in their vitriolic and discomfiting performances. Harrowing vignettes were needled out on guitar while Descloux yelped fragmented declarations in French and English.

Rosa Yemen recorded a single, self-titled EP at Bob Blank's Blank Tapes studio. In July 1978 it became ZE's fifth release. Descloux rejoiced, saying: "ZE knew [the

---

1. It's unclear whether the man she contacted was actually her biological father; Descloux's mother had also dated the man's brother, and neither man had been aware of Descloux's birth.

SAINT-FLORENT, CORSICA, 1985

"Those who refuse to get out of the
underground are often bitter and stubborn."

—LMD

EP] wouldn't go anywhere, that nobody would buy it, and they were just doing it and paying for it and it was *great*."

In February 1979, Descloux returned to Blank Tapes for 10 days to record her solo debut, *Press Color*. The record's fusion of no wave and disco was notably more melodic than *Rosa Yemen*, and the change in direction was partially the result of ZE's "vision of what their artists should be and how they should do things." Descloux's labelmate James Chance avers that the label was pushing disco on their artists but letting them interpret it however they wanted. In Descloux's case, this meant yoking her newfound love of African and funk music to disco's strong rhythmic foundations, while she pursued guitar tones that sounded nothing like rock.

Press Color was released as Descloux's first solo album, but it was originally intended to be a group effort. "It felt natural to put her name on it," says Esteban. "She was the main character." But she told a Belgian paper that there were songs on the record she didn't like, including her cover of Arthur Brown's "Fire." It's at this point that questions begin arise as to who was making the decisions. "Michel, from the very beginning, always saw her as his ticket to stardom, as his big star," says Seth Tillett, a former boyfriend. "She always didn't really give a fuck. If anyone was a reluctant singer, that was Lizzy. There's that famous photo of her in black and white, practically strangling herself with her guitar amp cord on stage—it's the perfect image for me about Lizzy's ambivalence."

Yet Descloux was adamant when a *Creem* journalist asked whether she felt exploited: "No, not at all. I mean, I write the music that I'm doing, I'm not only performing… I mean—I'm not just *used* by some *male* musician who's going to dress me up and have me to dance just to look sexy on stage and just be a support for some kind of music." But Esteban admits to pushing her so hard in the studio that they fought frequently. He wanted her to sing rather than yelp, imagining that he was encouraging her to reach her full capabilities, but *Press Color* shows her revelling in the potential of her naïve approach. *"I'll never have a golden throat!"* she whoops, leaping between high and low notes on every opposing syllable of "No Golden Throat."

"Right now I'm not at all a writer of words," she explained. "I'm using the words completely for what they sound like, how they fit with the rhythms. I'm not interested in writing a love song, or a political statement about what's happening with Ireland, like people are gonna listen to my lyrics and it's gonna *change* the *youth* of the *world*… What's beautiful is that I don't speak perfect English but I can get lost in the dictionary and just *discover* the words."

After *Press Color* was released, Descloux says she "did all the clubs in New York," first as support, then as headliner. Despite the practice, a feature in *New York Rocker* from July 1980 indicates that her performances of this material were hesitant in comparison to the unhinged Rosa Yemen shows that she had relished. Sally Dricks wrote: "It's frustrating to want to *goad* a performer as talented as Lizzy Mercier Descloux toward what only time, experience and confidence will make possible, but it won't be long before she learns to command that space before a crowd by pushing *herself* just a little bit further than she thinks she's able to do, further than she knows will make an easy return."

It's hard to find any indication that Descloux craved attention or adoration; she left Paris in order to escape the stultifying working-class life lived by her aunt and uncle, the latter of whom worked in the Renault factory by day and played boules at the Jardin des Tuileries after hours. By 1980, Descloux had become bored of New York's self-limiting attitude: "You get exhausted very quickly because there's no way of getting out of the club scene [...] You can be huge there and nothing in the rest of the world. Thousands of groups never get out, they try to play Boston and California but it's a disaster. Look at the Lounge Lizards, no label wants to sign them and they get the best crowds, sell the most tickets, it's been nearly two years. They said to me the other day that they reckon they earn $30 a week, so they are going to stop."

Likewise, she railed against indifferent audiences: "They stand there holding a beer. It's young Americans who come out on Saturday night because they're bored. You're just an attraction."

A chance to move on came when Island Records licensed ZE's catalog and label head Chris Blackwell invited Descloux to record in Compass Point Studios in Nassau on his dime. She readily accepted, having become a big fan of the African and Caribbean music she'd heard on compilations released by French label Ocora. Esteban assembled a band (including producer Steve Stanley and French synthesizer giant Wally Badarou), and recording began. Badarou describes the sessions as largely improvisation-based, with Descloux functioning as a "one-of-a-kind catalyst, enabling creative forces to blossom without any preconceived ideas. She simply had the kind of drive and charisma that would make anyone involved more focused on trespassing boundaries."

Released in 1981, the tightly wound *Mambo Nassau* is Descloux's greatest record: It bounces on the same kind of pancultural groove with which M.I.A. would make a name for herself decades later, blaring with the sound of city sirens reinterpreted by lusty brass. She yips in a kind of pidgin Franglais, unleashing joyous trills and impish taunts, and for the first time the vivid music on the record matches the sheer exuberance of her live performance. Talking Heads' *Fear of Music* was talked up for its Afro-beat cre-

dentials, but the music was fundamentally recognizable as New York art rock. As potentially commercial as it seems now, *Mambo Nassau* is an uncontainable, wild masterpiece that genuinely sounds like little else that was around at the time.

Despite the record's promise, its release was marred by chronic distribution problems and Esteban's departure from ZE (though he remained Descloux's de facto manager). "You spend eight months of your life making something, then at the end you realise it will never come out because three bankers are arguing over a bit of vinyl," Descloux said.

 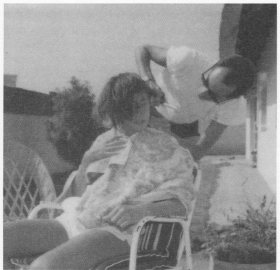

JOHANNESBURG, 1983

"Once I found myself with a guitar in my hands it was inevitable—I was committed to singing."

—LMD

With no distribution deal and two poorly selling albums, it was difficult for Descloux to secure another contract, but Alain Levy, then at CBS, liked her records and offered a deal. The move to CBS led journalists to ask pointedly whether she had sold out. Descloux refuted the accusations, reasoning that ZE was an imprint of the major-owned Island. For her, the very notion of selling out vindicated everything she thought about the underground: "The underground—that so often means that you just lack means [...] It was good at the time when I was doing my musical apprenticeship, but it doesn't interest me any more. Those who refuse to get out of the underground are often bitter and stubborn."

Descloux wanted to record in South Africa with black *mbaqanga* musicians in the midst of apartheid, despite the UN's cultural boycott: "It all came from one day when a friend played me some South African records that knocked me over [...] Straight away I said I wanted to work with these people. And voilà: it's a record of a meeting between different worlds, not just the story of a European woman who goes to Africa. I wasn't there to find the sound of tam-tams or the hissing of snakes, or, like an anthropologist, resuscitate ancient cave rhythms. Their music is very alive."

Uncertain, CBS funded demo sessions in Paris with producer Adam Kidron, but he and Descloux were unable to find the sound they wanted. Determined to get to South Africa, Mercier found reduced plane tickets and a cheap studio; CBS signed the check, and Descloux, Esteban, and Kidron—whom she was now dating—toured Africa before arriving in Soweto to record.

Initially, the *mbaqanga* musicians regarded her suspiciously. This was the aftermath of Malcolm McLaren's *Duck Rock*, on which he had sampled music from South Africa, South America, and the Caribbean without crediting some of the musicians—which landed him in court. However, after a week the musicians decided that Descloux's intentions were honorable and began to jam with her, though their collaboration had to remain within the studio. Descloux was shocked by the realities of apartheid: "You can't go to the cinema with a black person, sleep at their house, embrace them, dance with them in clubs [...] Racism exists everywhere. In New York, I have black friends who can't get a cab in the evening. But the terrible thing in South Africa is that racism is part of the system. There are white people, then Indians, then the Métis, and finally black people."

The resulting album, *Zulu Rock*, earned Descloux the Bus d'Acier award for Best French Rock Album of the Year (an accolade she found hilarious given how unlike French rock the album actually was) and spawned a hit single, "Mais Où Sont Passés Les Gazelles," an impressionistic protest song about apartheid based on her band's re-recording of the music of Obed Ngobeni and Kurhula Sisters' "Ku Hluvukile Eka Zete." She used the song's video shoot as an excuse to spend eight hours interviewing Soweto locals about their experiences of apartheid, intending to release it along with a book on her return home, though it never came out.

"I've always been aware of racism and intolerance, but the project very quickly became political," she said. "But I think being subtle is better than barbed wire and a black fist on the cover. The fact that the record exists is significant enough." She is more unequivocal on "Sun's Jive," however, singing of the Afrikaners, "They should go back and disappear forever / Where? The middle of nowhere / The bottom of the sea."

Unfortunately, her good intentions unravelled when it became clear that some of the South African source material had not been credited. "We listened to the top records in South Africa at the time, took the melodies, re-recorded them with a bunch of musicians and she just put French lyrics on top of them," says Kidron. Esteban refutes his claims: "Some songs are covers. The rest were studio jams. I made the deal with the musicians there and did the publishing there, everything was normal."

French monthly *Actuel* gave *Zulu Rock* a rave review one month, but on learning of the controversy, retracted it the next. Descloux said, "They accused me of having stolen traditional songs like Malcolm McLaren. It's not true—half of the music on this album is credited to its authors, and the other half is made up of popular music that I rearranged and re-adapted to such an extent that nobody has the right to put their name to it. Nobody would be able to recognize them, the songs have changed." (In this way, perhaps, she is as much the original Diplo as she is the original M.I.A.)

The incident tarnished the only small success of Descloux's career. She had gone to Soweto with good intentions and wanted to take the South African musicians on tour and then to New Orleans, to record an album fusing *mbaqanga* and Cajun music. CBS put up the money, but the Praetorian government wouldn't let the musicians leave. The project was shelved. Exhausted by the amount of promotion CBS made her do, Descloux disappeared for a while to Asia, where she was popular.

Alain Levy, Descloux's champion at CBS, left the company, which put her at the mercy of a major. Before he left, he gave her the money to go to Rio de Janeiro to record *One for the Soul* in 1986. It's a total sea change from the bright rhythms of her first three records; instead, "Lizzy sings the blues" says Kidron, who once again produced. A drug-ravaged Chet Baker gave one of his last recorded performances, imbuing the record with a mournful tone. Unlike its predecessors, *One for the Soul* has aged badly; Descloux is drowned out by the overblown '80s production. "I thought she could have sung better on this album," says Esteban, who stopped managing her after its release.

There are few interviews from this period, so it's hard to tell how Descloux felt about the record: fairly annoyed, one assumes, given that it went nowhere. But "she wasn't fed up musically," insists Mars' Mark Cunningham, who joined her for her final record, 1988's *Suspense*, which they recorded in England with producer John Brand. "She put herself into it 100 per cent, with no distractions from boyfriends or managers."

Where *One for the Soul* was unrecognizable as the same artist who once shrieked on stage with Rosa Yemen, there was more of Descloux in *Suspense*, which proved to be a happy marriage between her unconventional rhythms and the gated synths and snares of '80s production. The first single, "Gueules d'Amour," was another flop. "As soon as the label saw they didn't have a hit, they withdrew the promotion to reduce losses," says Cunningham. "They destroyed her career, in a sense, by burying the album."

It's almost incomprehensible that Descloux was allowed to release as many unsuccessful major label albums as she was. Nonetheless, she had grown accustomed to handsome recording budgets and label heads who were willing to finance her exotic excursions, so after *Suspense* was DOA, it's little surprise that slinking back to the underground held no appeal. She threw herself into painting, briefly coming out of musical retirement for 1995's "Matinée d'Ivresse" with Patti Smith. That same year she recorded an album for EMI, which was never released.[2]

It's difficult to piece together Descloux's movements during the last nine years of her life. One friend reports that she worked on a tourist boat on a tropical island and dated a stockbroker whom she didn't particularly like. She lived in Guadeloupe and later in Happonvilliers, France. In 2003 she was diagnosed with stage-three ovarian and colon cancer but refused conventional treatment. Determined not to die in a hospital, she spent time with Esteban at his home in the south of France, had a brief spell in a Parisian hospital, where she and Esteban said goodbye, and lived out her last weeks in Corsica, passing on April 20, 2004.

"The public were unmoved by her death and French newspapers barely mentioned it," says French journalist Simon Clair, who is writing a book on Descloux. France is not exactly rich with great musical exports (as John Lennon once put it, "French rock is like English wine"), so one would have expected the press to deify her. However, she and the French press perceived each other as being snobbish, and deserters never fare well. If her legacy wasn't recognized, her wake—which took place in CBGBs, organized by Richard Hell—demonstrated her influence. "It was really funny to see how many people felt they were totally possessed by Lizzy, how she was capable of making everyone feel that way," says Seth Tillett.

"Lizzy never thought she had something to prove," says Esteban. "I don't think she was ambitious in the pejorative sense. She didn't have that big ego to become a superstar."

Descloux was never jaded about her lack of recognition. For her, music was not about success but forward motion and a refusal to accept the limitations of genre, geography, or any other convention, choosing instead to live like an endless seed of mystery on the breeze. "I don't work in terms of fashions," she once said. "At the very limit I might contribute to creating them. But that isn't intentional." ✎

LAURA SNAPES *is a Contributing Editor at* Pitchfork.

2. After her death, Esteban bought the record back from EMI. It might be released later this year.

SWITZERLAND, 1984

"I think women have a certain sensibility that could make
them approach guitar in a beautiful way."

—LMD

DISCOGRAPHIE

ROSA YEMEN (ZE Records, 1978)

Released within a year of Descloux first picking up the guitar, *Rosa Yemen* thrives on its limitations. She and Didier Esteban construct menacing vignettes from just two guitars, one maintaining a tense, quivering two-note foundation while the other needles out a hysterical top end. There is no percussion save for the dub rhythm seemingly slapped out on a tub on "Decryptated," and although every song has essentially the same rhythm and structure, the EP's crudeness contributes to its harrowing atmosphere—helped, of course, by Descloux's rabid shrieks and declarations. "Fuck you, fucking," she seems to spit on "Herpes Simplex."

PRESS COLOR (ZE Records, 1979)

Where *Rosa Yemen* felt ad hoc and impulsive, *Press Color* is a significantly more refined record, having been made in ZE's no-wave-meets-disco mold. It develops Descloux's knack for making each of her records into its own distinct world. Arthur Brown's "Fire," the theme tune from *Mission: Impossible*, and a reprise of Peggy Lee's "Fever" as "Tumor" are reimagined as playfully sinister punk-funk songs, while the dubby screeds of originals "Wawa" and "Torso Corso" align her with the contemporary Bristol post-punk scene.

MAMBO NASSAU (CBS, 1981)

After the austere palettes of her first two records, *Mambo Nassau* explodes into vivid Caribbean color. Co-written by synth genius Wally Badarou, opener "Lady O K'pele" catalyses every aspect of the vanguard sound Descloux explores on the album: heavy thrusting bass, dub, bubbling samples, a male voice choir chanting in the background, punk-funk rhythms, and the kind of stuttering synths that William Onyeabor was thrilling Lagos with around the same time. Meanwhile, Descloux exclaims in joyous pidgin nonsense: "Kumar kumar! Chicken, braaaa!" "Milk Sheik" is a Nino Rota rip-off that sticks out like a sore thumb—sounding as if it should be swirling at the centre of a Parisian carousel rather than an island in the Bahamas—but a cover of Kool & The Gang's "Funky Stuff" is a better fit. "Nobody's watching in here / So what!" Descloux sings explosively.

ZULU ROCK (CBS, 1984)

Zulu Rock takes most of the angles and aggression out of Descloux's music, leaving in its wake this sunny, lapping stream of a record. It is a strangely captivating mix of traditions: The frequent presence of accordion ties together one of France's defining sounds with that of the Dutch Boers, who settled in South Africa in the 18th century, and whose music became absorbed into *mbaqanga*. Here its oompah rhythm gives *Zulu Rock* a capering, winningly cartoonish feel, decorated by the drip-dripping guitar and organ rhythms. Descloux sings a lot, commemorating free spirits and sex while decrying oppression, represented here in the form of the white Afrikaners. "As far as color line, I'll go for color blind," she sings on "Wakwazulu Kwezizulu Rock."

ONE FOR THE SOUL (CBS, 1986)

Once Descloux and her cohort landed in Rio de Janeiro for the recording of her fourth album, they tracked down Chet Baker at a local jazz festival and persuaded him to appear on the record. It's hard to tell whether his criminal underuse on *One for the Soul* is due to his poor health (he died two years later) or the abject lack of direction on the record. Regardless, it's Descloux's first album that can (to its detriment) be pinned to a specific point in time. Its version of the blues is kitschy and overwhelms her weak singing, which wasn't suited to seduction. Her directionlessness is spelled out on the leery "God-Spell Me Wrong": "I don't know my heart from my head / Don't know my ups from my down."

SUSPENSE (Polygram, 1988)

Descloux rediscovers—or is given back—her rhythm on what would become her final record, one which contains moments of promise amid production decisions that make no sense. Although she is singing stronger here than on *One for the Soul*, she sounds lost inside swampy piano ballads like "The Long Goodbye" and "Echec et Mat." Polygram were breathing down producer John Brand's neck for a hit, so most of the songs here are tarted up with late-1980s sonic tropes—gated snares, xylophone filigrees—which work trememndously on "Gueule d'Amour," "Vroom, C'est la Voie Lactée," and "2 Femmes à la Mer," recalling Talk Talk's *Spirit of Eden*, also released that year.

WORKS CITED

Télémoustique, June 28, 1984. *Rock News*, May 1976. *La Dépêche*, March 1984. *Creem*, May 1980. *New York Rocker*, July/August 1980. Undated clip from *Invitation Rock & Folk*, August 1980. *Télépro*, 1984. *Rock*, 1984. *Chanson*, 1984. *Le Soir*, April 27, 1984. *Le Quotidien*, August 1984. *Nice Matin*, April 1984

Debbie Harry in her apartment on 58ᵗʰ Street in New York City in the early '80s.
PHOTO BY CHRIS STEIN

The Chuck Taylor All Star

Made by Patti Smith

★CONVERSE
Made by you